Whole Armor of Marriage

CAROLINE JENS

A companion to

Whole Armor of Marriage, 40 Day Couples Journal

Cover by Dana Breunig, Milwaukee, Wisconsin
Edit by Christina Miller, Mentor's Pen Editorial

THE WHOLE ARMOR OF MARRIAGE

Website: www.wholearmorministry.com

ISBN-13: 978-0615897066
ISBN-10: 0615897061

This book is dedicated to...

My husband, Daniel Jens, for allowing me to write transparently to the world about our relationship, our trials, and our victories. I feel so blessed to have met this man who led me to Christ, and I owe him my life for introducing me to the EXPERIENCE of God.

I am forever humbled and changed because of the four-year experience he gave me as an Army wife in Fort Hood, Texas. It was from this life-changing season of our lives that the Whole Armor of Marriage was birthed.

You've shown me dreams are obtainable if you have the faith and determination to achieve them. You turned my childhood dream into a reality by miraculously giving me a beautiful lake home. This was something I never thought could happen in my life, but you remained determined and, as usual, achieved it. You are such an inspiration!

We've been through many valleys and mountaintop experiences, yet we have continued to stay steadfast and in love with each other and with God. You are my soul mate and my head of household.

TABLE OF CONTENTS

INTRODUCTION

Writing a book on marriage can be a scary task. Who can claim to be an expert on marriage? What can I write about that is dramatically different from any other marriage book currently in circulation? How will I be affected personally when areas of my own life are exposed to anyone who reads this book? I pondered all those questions, especially about sharing personal stories that even my closest family members may not know of.

My first attempt at writing *Whole Armor of Marriage* was directed specifically toward military families experiencing deployment or long separations. When I wrote the military edition of *Whole Armor of Marriage*, I vowed to be transparent about my life. Having experienced the up and down sides to being an army wife, I knew the importance of sharing what I'd learned. My husband and I must have stayed together for a reason, and our story of how we kept our marriage alive had to be told.

Today, I write with that same commitment to being honest and transparent about my experience with marriage. Throughout *Whole Armor of Marriage*, I will do my best to provide stories of real trials we faced and focus on how we overcame those trials. I have many different experiences to draw from since my marriage has not only survived four years in the Army, fifteen months of a deployment to Iraq, half of a year on a reality television show, and two years of separation due to traveling for music, post-traumatic stress disorder (PTSD), but it has also survived battles with addictions. Addictions so horrifying and controlling, that most people couldn't fathom its destruction.

Because of love and God's intervention, my husband and I remain together, mutually focused, God-centered, and ministry-driven. It has not been easy, but I feel we have gone through these experiences so I could put them on paper and we could speak about them to help others.

While reading *Whole Armor of Marriage*, consider trying some of the tools that have worked in our marriage. Learn to rely on the spiritual armor of marriage and keep the life-long commitment of marriage to your spouse. Wouldn't it be wonderful if we could be the generation that decides to remake a commitment to marriage and this sovereign contract before God? We challenge you to join us on the journey and commit to a happy, long-lasting, and fruitful marriage.

How to Get the Most out of This Book

Whole Armor of Marriage was written to help families grow stronger and to last the test of time. Within this book, you'll find valuable concepts my husband and I currently use, and have used, throughout the course of our marriage. We've experienced ups and downs in our relationship, and we learned how to apply spiritual armor daily, which protected our marriage from becoming a divorce statistic.

We all need to protect and value our marriages as priceless treasures. When you view your marriage in this light—as a priceless treasure— you will want to do whatever you can, at all cost, to keep it safe.

As you continue to read *Whole Armor of Marriage*, consider the daily protection you can hold onto that will keep yourself and your family secure. I encourage you and your spouse to read this book with an open heart and mind. To get you focused on the topic right from the start, each chapter will begin with a Focus Verse and Focus Thought. Take the time to read and reflect on each before reading the chapter material. Alternatively, each chapter will end with Time to Engage activities, designed to challenge you and your spouse to evaluate your relationship. The Time to Engage activity is broken into three sections: Questions for Reflection, A Call to Action and Time with God. The reflection questions are meant to help you and your spouse identify strong and weak areas in your marriage. The Call to Action section has several items for you to complete. It will teach you hands-on methods of applying the armor you learned about in that chapter. Finally, the Time with God section will encourage you to spend time with God, reflecting on what you've learned.

To help tighten the spiritual armor explored in *Whole Armor of Marriage*, utilize the corresponding forty-day journal. This journal is designed to encourage couples to reflect on and challenge themselves to growing deeper in applying each piece of spiritual armor.

Finally, to get the most out of this book, you and your spouse must adopt an attitude of commitment and persistence in your journey toward improving and strengthening your marriage. This commitment must be impenetrable, allowing nothing and no one, including yourself, to keep you from persisting in strengthening your marriage.

Get committed, get focused, and get ready to enjoy life with your spouse!

CHAPTER ONE: THE ARMOR

Focus Thought: Take up the whole armor each day.

Focus Verse: "Therefore take up the whole armor of God, that you may be able to withstand in the evil day, and having done all, to stand" (Ephesians 6:13).

Man meets Woman

Eyes meet for the first time, which makes the hearts of this unsuspecting pair quiver. The fire of a new relationship has ignited. With new relationships come times of new experiences, new memories, and new hope.

As the relationship progresses past the initial attraction, serious decisions must be confronted. Is this person on the same page as I am spiritually? Do they have the same financial goals? Do they believe marriage is a lifetime commitment that should not be broken?

Often, we enter into marriage without answering those key questions. We generally go into marriage blindly, or we intentionally put blinders on because we desire the company of another, and the fear of loneliness is worse than the fear of being in a mismatched marriage.

Fast-forward this relationship five years. Unless you have learned to communicate, unconditionally show love, withhold resentment, and treat your spouse with respect, divorce may be a topic of consideration. At this point, loneliness may take over the relationship even though fear of loneliness was partly why you entered into this relationship in the first place.

A slow fade begins with small actions on the part of both the husband and the wife. At this point, other things have become priority over their spouse. These are times when a new friend turns into a lover. Additions of new hobbies consume your time. Whatever action takes place, hopelessness for the lifetime commitment of marriage becomes a reality.

There's a way to combat this ever-growing trend. Applying the whole armor of marriage each day and keeping God centered through it all, you will have everlasting power throughout the years of your marriage. Remaining embedded in faith, we put our marriage in God's hands. This commitment to God and our spouse lets the adversary know we will not be defeated. Along with committing to a life directed by faith, our families must have a passion to save our marriages at all cost. Passion and commitment, rooted in faith, are ingredients for a healthy and resilient marriage.

Does this sound like you? Are you passionate about your marriage? Are you willing to learn and apply proven principles to your marriage? Are you open to learning the same basic fundamental principles my husband and I rely on each day? Once you dive into these principles, you and your spouse may feel outside your comfort zone, especially if your relationship currently does not include a close walk with God. I want to encourage you not to let this keep you from learning some basic principles that will make your relationship with your spouse much more satisfying.

Most of the precepts in this book are basic marriage principles. I have expanded them to include keeping God as the foundation of your relationship. This spiritual foundation will provide your marriage and your family with added strength to overcome obstacles and keep joy in your everyday life.

Understanding the Whole Armor of God

If someone asked you if marriage was easy, what would you say? Marriage is like a fairy-tale? Would you be confident enough in your marriage to say you don't need to work on it at all? Probably not!

I'm sure most of us would admit that marriage is hard work. Consider for a moment how hard marriage is, and then factor in additional obstacles. What if your spouse has become distant over the year(s)? What if one of you lost your job and your finances are falling apart? What if your spouse has an ever-growing addiction? What would your answer be in that case? I imagine you would say, "Not only is it hard, but it feels impossible at times!"

Applying the Armor: A Personal Story

My husband and I have dealt with his addiction for most of our relationship. Historically, when things are going wonderfully and all the pieces in our lives are in the right place, my husband will fall. This kind of fall is so intense it affects our relationship, our household, our finances, and our ministry. Learning to pick those pieces back up is very difficult, and at one time in our journey, it felt impossible. October, 2010 was the worst fall in the history of our marriage. At this point he had built up everything he wanted in life. Not only did he obtain his musical dreams, but he had finally started winning back the respect of a lot of people who once abandoned him.

For me, the effects of this fall almost prevented me from recovering. Nearing a nervous breakdown, I pondered a horrifying question: "If he could fall when he had "everything," what could ever stop this from happening again?" This fall left me hopeless for the first time in our marriage.

My God had different plans, however. Failing in this marriage was not an option. The words of a guest evangelist, three days after the fall, reminded me not to let the lion devour our household. The devil comes to steal, kill, and destroy, and we were perfect prey. I came home from hearing that message and immediately recommitted to my marriage. I had to commit to being all-in, unwavering, and unstoppable.

By putting God back at the center of our relationship, we were able to have full restoration of our marriage, and many amazing miracles happened because of it. We became mentors for the college and career group at our church, my husband landed an amazing job, he went back to college, we gained custody of his son, and finally, we purchased my dream home on a lake. Not only did ALL these miracles happen, but they all happened in less than a year of almost giving up and walking away from my commitment to marriage.

Full restoration of our marriage not only required us to commit, but it also required us to be disciplined in applying the whole armor of God. The armor God provides is not a joke or myth. His armor is available to anyone who believes in His power and the authority of being a chosen child of the King. The armor, when applied daily, helps us achieve spiritual milestones that our flesh would only hinder.

Without the ability or understanding of how to apply the armor in your marriage, the strain of insecurity, along with fear or loss of hope, can be too much to handle. This tension, along with life's normal hiccups, can make families vulnerable to attacks.

To get a clear understanding of the power of God's spiritual armor, you must first understand the biblical principle of the whole armor of God. The focus verse at the start of this chapter references this principle. If you continue to read further in Ephesians 6, you'll receive clear instruction from God on how to stand protected from life's attacks:

> *Stand therefore, having girded your waist with truth, having put on the breastplate of righteousness, and having shod your feet with the preparation of the gospel of peace; above all, taking the shield of faith with which you will be able to quench all the fiery darts of the wicked one. And take the helmet of salvation, and the sword of the Spirit, which is the word of God. (Ephesians 6:14-17)*

We can use the teaching in Ephesians to prepare ourselves spiritually from the moment we awake in the morning. This imagery can keep us focused and on the right path each day. The illustrations can be explained in short as:

- *Belt (Girdle):* The belt reminds us to stay tied in with truth.

- *Breastplate:* The breastplate protects us from sin and keeps us on a righteousness path.

- *Shoes:* The shoes remind us to stand firm in the Gospel and to preach it everywhere.

- *Shield:* The shield demonstrates our faith and the protection faith will bring us.

- *Helmet:* The helmet depicts the safeguard we must place on our minds every day to protect our thoughts. If we are filled with worry, fear, and doubt, we will take our minds off Jesus.

- *Sword:* The sword of the Spirit is God's Word and is the ultimate protection we hold onto. There is power behind God's Word. Become familiar with it so we can use it in battle and to edify others.

The scripture that teaches on the whole armor of God provides details on how to apply these various types of protection daily so we can stand strong as Christians. In addition to this armor, we are taught to pray, be watchful, and persevere. Life is difficult for all of us at various points and seasons. Marriage can prove more difficult each day. We are always vulnerable to life's attacks, and we must believe there is a way to protect ourselves. By applying the biblical principles described in Ephesians and continually strengthening our relationship with God, we can overcome all trials that come our way.

To accomplish this, we must discipline ourselves not to leave our bedsides without talking to God and asking Him to help us through the day. I encourage you to have a conversation with God before your feet hit the floor. Praise Him for waking you up and thank Him for what He plans to do for you that day.

Understanding the Whole Armor of Marriage

How does the whole armor of God apply to marriage, and can those same principles transform your relationship with your spouse? More important, how is it possible to incorporate all those principles into our busy lives? My husband and I used the whole armor of God scripture and transformed it to help with our marriage as we began to struggle during my husband's first deployment to Iraq. Prior to that time, we were used to having a close, interactive relationship, full of communication. Extended time apart hindered that piece we valued dearly.

As we labored to adjust, we found we were working not only to keep the relationship alive, but to also keep our marriage intact. All around us, soldiers' marriages were failing and falling apart. News of another broken home became overwhelmingly common as the deployment progressed. The weight of divorce news was unbearable and depressing. Whether or not the couple had issues before the spouse left for war, marriages were falling apart for all kinds of reasons. Spending time apart, unprepared and naïve did not help any marriage— including ours.

My husband and I needed to take drastic action fast before we became a statistic. We turned to the one thing we knew would offer us guidance: the Word of God. As we dove deeper and deeper into scripture, we came upon the whole armor of God. Though we had not always been faithful in daily applying it, we realized the power behind it.

With the "whole armor of God" principles in mind, my husband and I formed an elaborate plan to protect our marriage. We took the protection from Ephesians chapter six and developed a way to apply it specifically to our marriage. From this, the *Whole Armor of Marriage* plan evolved. It requires the husband and wife to apply similar pieces of spiritual armor at the start of each day to protect their home. Though the armor imagery is the same, the meaning behind each piece is specifically directed toward enhancing your marital experience. Let's take a closer look at the pieces of the whole armor of marriage and see God's plan.

- *The Belt: Stay fastened to each other and to God.* Keeping God as the center ("oneness") of your relationship will aid with trust issues, help keep priorities focused, provide direction in your lives, and encourage love between you and your spouse.

- *The Breastplate: Protect your heart by loving the people around you and receiving the love shown to you.* Respecting and loving your spouse sounds like common sense, but most relationships suffer because one spouse may feel as if the other has stopped doing it. Show encouragement and love to your spouse.

- *The Shoes: Have the heart of a servant and wash the feet of the one you love.* Selflessness will go miles when you put your spouse's needs before your own. Demonstrating your love by putting the other first will bring peace in your household because love will prevent resentment.

- *The Shield: God will protect you as long as you remain disciplined in carrying the shield of prayer.* Pray daily for a hedge of protection around your family. The shield of prayer is always crucial to providing peace in your household and for protection for your spouse and your children.

- *The Helmet: Communicating and knowing what the other is thinking will protect your mind from doubt and fear.* Communicating with your spouse and family requires daily effort, but it will protect you from unneeded arguments. There should be no secrets in a marriage!

- *The Sword: The tongue is a sword that can easily edify someone or crush them completely.* Encouraging words will eliminate the chance of hurtful comments or regrettable actions. We must encourage with our tongues, not pierce with them. Use the sword as protection, not as a weapon!

Overall, we agreed that if we focused on these key attributes each day, we would have a better chance of living a happy and victorious marriage. Marriage calls for support, strength, determination, encouragement, compassion, and most important, love. I assure you, it's possible to have a thriving and happy marriage even after five, ten, fifteen years of marriage. It's possible to follow through with the commitment "till death do you part." Our marriage is a testament to God's plan keeping you on a solid foundation.

Persistence

Persistence plays a crucial role in the success of any marriage. A healthy and long-lasting marriage requires you to be persistent in your actions, deeds, and commitment. In today's society, marriage is expendable. This mentality can lead relationships straight toward divorce when things get tough. At all cost, husbands and wives must strive to be persistent in marriage. This means we have made a conscious decision not to give up when things get tough.

Making it through the tough times is what my husband and I describe as the "mountaintop" experience. When things are going great between us, we consider ourselves at the top of the mountain, enjoying life. While on the mountaintop, we rarely argue, we strive toward focused goals, and life generally goes our way. When things are not going so well, however, we say we are in the valley. We struggle to remain on the same page. Life in general seems like a chore we are doing alone. We would love to live at the top of the mountain throughout the entire course of our relationship, but that is not realistic. We'll always have ups and downs, no matter how close we walk to God.

Since we can't live on the mountaintop every day, we must be persistent in our journey with each other. This persistence is crucial as we go through the valley and the trials. The whole armor of marriage, coupled with persistence, is the utmost survival tool!

You'll need to work together diligently and apply the whole armor, especially in the valley. Be encouraged and stand strong in your marriage. Don't give up just because life gets hard. You'll learn to handle more obstacles as seasons change. So much joy can be achieved in a marriage if you and your spouse remain persistent!

Make the Choice!

Let's make the choice, pick up the armor, and apply it. Looking at the armor won't protect you. Nor can you leave it lying around and be protected. It requires effort by both you and your spouse. You will have to make the choice to apply this protection each day.

However, don't be discouraged if you are not always victorious in picking up your armor. My husband and I are not always successful in applying our armor in our marriage. We are not perfect creatures. At times, one or both of you will fail. If one falls, keep encouraging them, even if they have fallen several times.

This can be the most challenging and influential decision you can make! If one of you becomes too relaxed in your marriage or your walk with God, the other must encourage continued growth. For this to work, we must be open to correction from our spouse. We must also be accountable to each other for our actions and inactions. Your commitment to a healthy marriage, especially one grounded in faith, will ultimately strengthen the other, not weaken them.

The following chapters will explain each piece of armor in detail and give you tools to keep your family strong. Consider these tools and work on applying them as a couple. If you're not strong in your faith or active in the church, take heart anyway. The intention of this book is not to discuss religious denominations or to make you feel guilty about your walk with God. It is meant to challenge you in your relationship with your spouse and teach you ways to make your life together better!

We don't have to be like the rest of the world and slowly lose interest in our spouse. Our marriages do not have to be destined to fail. We can have strong, long-lasting, loving relationships throughout their entirety. I challenge you and your spouse to look at your marriage and its current direction. Make a vow to find joy in each other and the life you share. I'm not promising each day will be filled with sunshine and chirping birds or that you'll have no financial problems or hurtful situations. I do, however, believe relationships can be strong enough to endure when problems try to turn you off course. Relationships can be joyful and loving and can persist for a lifetime.

Always be humble and gentle. Be patient with each other, making allowances for each other's faults because of your love. (Ephesians 4:2)

TIME TO ENGAGE

This book is intended to help you and your spouse learn how to protect your marriage. The union in marriage must not be taken lightly. We are required to hold onto the commitment we made at the altar and not waiver. Husbands and wives, it's time to profess that you intend to spend the rest of your lives with the person you fell in love with.

Questions for Reflection

- What attributes of your marriage do you feel are strong? Discuss with your spouse the ways you can use those strengths when going to battle during difficult times in your relationship or just in your daily life.

- What attributes of your marriage do you feel are weak? How can you personally help improve those weak areas of your marriage?

- Of the various pieces of armor discussed in this chapter, which do you think will be the easiest to apply and why? Which will be the hardest to apply and why?

A Call to Action

- Write your spouse a letter telling why you are reading this book and what you hope to get out of it. Give your letter to your spouse before you finish reading this book

- Commit to praying at least five minutes each morning if that is not something you already do.

- List two activities you will do from now until the end of this book to improve your relationship with your spouse. Implement them immediately with or without your spouse knowing the motive.

Time with God

- Proverbs 16:16: *"How much better to get wisdom than gold! And to get understanding is to be chosen rather than silver."*

- James 1:4: *"But let patience have its perfect work, that you may be perfect and complete, lacking nothing."*

CHAPTER TWO: THE BELT

Focus Thought: Stay fastened to each other and to God.

Focus Verse: "So then, they are no longer two but one flesh. Therefore what God has joined together, let not man separate" (Matthew 19:6).

Belt of Oneness

Imagine having loose pants and no belt. What happens? You may feel "not quite together" and less confident. How about when the belt is fastened tight around your waist? Don't you immediately feel complete and presentable? Sometimes our relationship with our spouse and even with God can seem "not quite together." Fastening ourselves with God and our spouse will ensure a strong marriage.

However, we must buckle this belt properly and in order. Both husband and wife must put God first in their lives and their spouse second. In doing this, you can create an impenetrable oneness between yourself, your spouse, and God. This oneness is the belt that will securely hold your marriage, keeping you strong and together, able to withstand storms.

It may sound confusing or even selfish to put anything before your spouse. But we need to put God in the center of the relationship in order to protect ourselves from life's attacks. Once you gain an understanding of oneness in marriage, that unity will act like a belt, keeping your marriage fastened together so nothing can take it down. Oneness fastens the marriage tight because we consult God in every decision, we pray to God in every trial, and we thank God in every joy.

Consulting with God on every decision and turning to Him during trials and joyful times will reduce, if not eliminate, trust issues. This will keep priorities focused, provide direction in your life, and encourage love between you and your spouse. Imagine knowing your spouse consulted with God before making a crucial decision. Wouldn't that give you a sense of comfort? Now, imagine knowing your spouse is committed to putting God first in your lives. Wouldn't you feel reassured by the disciplines your spouse is trying to maintain so God can be first? We can develop such love, confidence, and strength when both husband and wife put God before the other.

Don't fret or worry. Instead of worrying, pray. Let petitions and praises shape your worries into prayers, letting God know your concerns. Before you know it, a sense of God's wholeness, everything

coming together for good, will come and settle you down. It's wonderful

what happens when Christ displaces worry at the center of your life.

(Philippians 4:6-7)

Keep God First and Centered

How do we keep God the center of each day, especially when society teaches us to look out for ourselves? This is done by starting and ending with the unbreakable commitment to put God at the center of each decision and to put our relationship with Him before all else. To do this, we start each day in prayer and in reading of His Word. Putting communication with God before all else takes a lot of discipline. However, this discipline will provide a strong connection with God and a much-needed balance in our lives and marriages.

His Word will direct your steps and shine light on any areas in your life that aren't in line with the walk God desires from you. Now consider sharing these moments with your spouse. You can enhance your daily prayer and reading by connecting with your spouse during these intimate experiences with God.

Learning Oneness: A Personal Story

One weekend during my husband's deployment to Iraq, I realized I was miserable. I spent every waking moment concentrating on myself, my loneliness, and all the things I thought I was missing out on. I spent many drawn-out nights feeling sorry for myself, convinced that no one cared what I was going through. Every Sunday, I went to church and put on the best mask I could, pretending I was fine.

I had to do this because it got to the point that every time I went to church, I was sad. How could I call myself a Christian, a child of God, if I couldn't find joy and happiness while surrounded by His people?

Attending church with my husband has always been one of my favorite activities. Seeing my husband live for God has brought me so much peace. Sitting alone in church, week after week, made this once-joyful experience a dreaded endeavor.

At night, I lay awake on the couch because I couldn't sleep in our bed. I spent each night in a partial state of sleep in case the instant-messenger buzzed, signaling a two a.m. note from my husband as he arrived back to camp after a mission. I kept my phone close to my ear so I wouldn't miss a call or text from him. Many army wives spend deployments like this. This loneliness causes some to look elsewhere for love, whether in the form of alcohol, drugs, or *adultery. The Holy Spirit inside me kept me from looking to those places to fill*

my void. My loneliness and sadness, however, never seemed to go away.

As days turned into months and I continued to dwell on my

loneliness, I did more than just hurt myself. Almost every time my husband

and I talked, we expressed only our sadness instead of enjoying the time we had

together on the phone. Something had to change. I was creating unneeded stress

for my husband, and in Iraq, that could get him or his fellow soldiers killed.

Consumed with myself and filled with loneliness and desperation, I

finally understood why I needed God to be the center of it all. I recalled my

pastor saying that we must make God first every day and involve Him in every

decision. Pastor said that if we focus on God's will and God's desires, then we

will spend less time focusing on selfish needs.

If, as a couple, you keep God in the center of each day and each

decision, you'll spend less time focusing on things that can strain a marriage.

Oneness between you, your spouse, and God will eliminate selfish desires and

the temptation of depression.

As you read in my personal story, I struggled in a number of

areas. I am grateful that God demonstrated His love for me so clearly

and gently that day. This is one of the reasons I challenge you to put

26

God in the center of your relationship. He is good to those who put His will first. We must trust His plan for us and use this trust to get through each day. Our families depend on us to hear God.

Immerse yourself in the presence of God, knowing that nothing can disturb or harm you. Allow yourself to experience joy and peace beyond understanding. Concentrate on God and allow yourself no opportunity to entertain distressing, worrisome thoughts. Then those emotions will pale in comparison to the magnificence of God.

I encourage you to immerse yourself in His love. Experience the deep sense of affection God has for you, and you will desire with all your heart to give that back to Him. Grasping the extent of His love allowed me to wake up each morning focusing on Him. Starting my day with my eyes on God strengthened my adoration and resolve toward my husband. My eyes were turned off myself, and my heart was open to love again. I was no longer consumed by fear and worry. I was free!

My husband noticed these changes, especially my new strength. Because of these changes, my husband rededicated his days to God. He now focuses on our oneness. Our relationship was strengthened and the time apart was no longer as fragile. We found joy in our days even though we were apart. Miles became inches as we shared our daily experiences with our Creator during our conversations. This was the turning point of my husband's tour in Iraq. Our marriage survived while others crumbled around us. The oneness we shared with God and each other was like a shield of armor we applied each day to protect our marriage.

Today, I pull from those days of that dreaded time apart. The experience of not knowing whether my spouse would return has become a benchmark for today's trials. Nothing life can throw at me can get as stressful as those fifteen months. Our ability to pull through, still happily married after such a dramatic separation, is something we are very proud of. It was all God and all because we kept Him the highest priority in our marriage.

Barriers to Oneness

It is important to recognize that certain barriers can hinder finding oneness between you, your spouse, and God. My husband and I encountered several of these barriers. Once you recognize the issues that hinder you as a couple, you can create an action plan to address them.

Those barriers to oneness might include:

- Selfishness

- Pride and self-love

- Idols

- Negativity

- Expectation

- Confrontation

Selfishness: Selfishness is all about putting yourself first. If you expect to have a relationship centered around God and with your spouse, you must guard against selfish needs. Don't get me wrong; your needs do count and are important! Having needs, desires, and dreams does not make you selfish. On the contrary, we all need goals, dreams, and desires. But if we put them before the protection of our marriage, selfishness will sneak into the relationship.

Oneness demands that you spend time thinking about your spouse's needs and God's desires. Once you learn to look to God each day for guidance and the right spirit, it will be much easier to think of others before yourself. You also need to protect your love for your spouse and God. In the next chapter, you will read about the breastplate of love. This breastplate will teach you how to protect your love. If you have love, it is much easier to sacrifice and put others before yourself.

Protecting this love is imperative to keeping our belt of oneness from being hindered. Love keeps us from selfishness and therefore keeps our belt fastened in our relationship.

Pride and Self-love: Pride and self-love can propel your ego in front of your spouse's needs. If you are prideful, you might have a tendency to believe things should be done for you or decisions should revolve around you. How can you create oneness in your relationship when you feel you should be set above others? Humility is a trait most of us need to learn. As you become more humble, even in your thoughts and your heart, you can break the barrier of pride.

Imagine thinking you should not have to do things around the house because you're the male of the family. What kind of tension will that create in your relationship? I suspect your wife will not feel appreciated if you demonstrate this type of demeanor.

Now imagine treating God in the same way. What would happen if we were determined to make a critical family decision without consulting God or our spouse first? Wouldn't that create a lot of unneeded tension within the household? These types of prideful decisions and actions build barriers to oneness in our relationships.

Idols: Idols can be deceiving. We may have a few and not realize it. An idol is anything you put before God. Idols will erect barriers to oneness in your relationship. If you spend the majority of your time on certain activities and at times put them ahead of prayer and other spiritual disciplines, then they become idols.

Our idols can have severe effects on our walk with God. We can also have idols that come before our spouse, and this can also cause tremendous problems in a marriage. Examples of idols are putting your friends before your spouse on a regular basis or watching television instead of talking with your spouse. These types of distractions can take a toll on a marriage. All too often, idols lower the level of intimacy you and your spouse share.

Negativity: Negativity can unfasten the belt of oneness in your marriage. If one or both spouses are always negative, it will be hard to have a joyful marriage. At all costs, try to prevent a pessimistic outlook.

Be encouraging and supportive to each other, and you'll have no room left for negativity.

Waking up each day to a gloomy spouse can have severe effects on a relationship. If your spouse has an issue with a negative outlook, you may need to sit them down and have a serious one-on-one talk. Be encouraging and compassionate when confronting a negative spouse. Generally, a negative person can show signs of negativity because they are not happy with their life or themselves, or they have lost hope. Perhaps their job has become very stressful. These are serious issues, and if you confront them too harshly or with the wrong spirit, you can cause more harm. Be gentle and compassionate.

Depression: A Personal Story

I remember feeling so depressed at one point in my life, I asked God to take me. I allowed the negativity in my life to take control of my mind and heart. I felt lost and alone. Things had escalated to this point because I was upset with some decisions I had recently made. In addition to those decisions, it was a time when my husband was traveling a lot with his music. I feared a lot when he traveled, because in my mind, I couldn't protect him from the world and his addiction.

When I reached this point of no hope, I finally got the courage to confide in a close friend of mine. I cried on the phone, explaining what I just asked God to do. I explained the decisions I had made, the fear I was feeling, and the hopelessness in my heart. It took that confession to a praying friend to help me get through a difficult time.

Learning to trust God with your life and future will help to lessen the chance for negativity to seep into your mind and heart. How can you be negative when you know God has your life in His hands? Do you believe God has your best interest in mind? Negativity can be the result of believing no one cares for you. If you suffer from negativity, take time to look deeply into your relationship with God. You may need to find peace in trusting God to help you overcome.

Expectation: Expectation can crush oneness because of the resentment and anxiety it can cultivate. Your spouse may not measure up to your expectations, and that can be a definite let-down. We will always fail to some degree. Unrealistic or demanding expectations can be fatal to a marriage. We can make our spouse feel like a constant failure if we always throw our expectation in their face. If you have high expectations, work on being honest with yourself.

This is an area I personally have to work at. I make conscious decisions to control my level of expectation every day. If I don't control this natural behavior of mine, I tend to overpower my spouse with too many demands. This type of behavior is not motivating and is not attractive.

If you are on the receiving end of these expectations, I encourage you to have a serious conversation with your spouse. Let them know how you feel when those expectations are forced upon you. Be compassionate and gentle when sharing your feelings. Learning how to communicate through these barriers is important to their resolution. My husband and I have spent many conversations learning how to communicate through this specific barrier. Be disciplined to hear your spouse and listen to their needs. Be open to change and be open to receiving criticism.

Our expectations of God can build a barrier to oneness with Him. Though God is the only one who will never fail us, we sometimes believe He does. If we ask Him for healing, financial blessing, or some other miracle but don't receive it during our timeframe, then we might be disappointed and even blame God. Don't fall into the misconception that if you are a Christian, nothing bad will ever happen to you. We all experience good and bad in our lives for many reasons. Instead of being disappointed because our expectation wasn't met, submerse yourself in prayer, finding the lesson you can learn from it. Spend time thanking God for the trial He has trusted you with. Imagine praising God for the bad things you go through. His trust in you is priceless, so thank Him for it every day. Hold onto the truth that God never fails. As humans, we will, and you will be more empathetic when someone fails you.

Confrontation: Confrontation can cause hurt feelings. If the confrontation escalates too much, it can have a lasting impact on a relationship. Confrontation comes in many forms and can arise for many reasons, but the outcome is almost always the same.

If confrontation is abundant in a marriage, it tends to build and may cause resentment and feelings of dislike. It's nearly impossible to feel close to a hostile person. Not only will the oneness be harder to achieve, but your relationship with God may also suffer. This can be especially true if you are the one who usually leads the confrontation. You may have feelings of guilt afterward that, if not dealt with, might build up and cause you to drift away from God. This is because our feelings of unworthiness make us less likely to talk with Him.

We must learn to take time out in prayer when confrontation is brewing so we can save our marriage from unneeded arguments. We must also remember to show respect to our spouse. Doing these simple things will limit the chance of saying something hurtful during a confrontation.

Fasten Up!

The focus verse at the start of this chapter states, "So they are no longer two, but one." This means that husbands and wives are no longer independent in actions or thoughts. We should always come together with our spouse and not act independently. This type of oneness seems to have disappeared in today's marriages. As you look around at friends and family, you'll see that many have their own bank accounts. They have separate goals, different schedules, and even separate dinner hours.

How can we become one with our spouse and with God if we continue to hold onto certain areas of our lives? Spend time reviewing your relationship and identifying areas that cause barriers to oneness. Enjoy being molded together as one! If you have never taken that approach with your spouse, I encourage you to develop this into your relationship. On the other hand, if you have lost this sense of oneness, work at rebuilding it.

Make the choice as a couple to put God in the center of your relationship so you can share oneness. In addition to making the choice, be aware of the various barriers that may hinder this oneness. Marriage in general is difficult. The obstacles families face make our marriages even more fragile. Take time each day to fasten the belt of oneness in your marriage. As a couple, learn to put God at the center. Our families can be stronger than ever if we stand fastened with our Creator. Life will not be perfect and without trial; however, you will be fastened to the ones you love as you conquer each obstacle.

TIME TO ENGAGE

The Belt of Oneness imagery is designed to help you visually perceive what a relationship fastened together by God would look like. He is the One who keeps us together. If we go through life fastened to our spouse and to God, we will become compassionate, loving, joyful, patient, and much more. Though we may not have all those qualities today, as we grow closer to God, we develop them. Learn to put God at the center of your relationship and see how that one change will take your relationship to a new level. When you marry, you are no longer independent, but you are one with your spouse. I encourage you to include God in that relationship!

Questions for Reflection

- What barriers hinder you from achieving oneness with God and your spouse?

- What type of conflict is in your relationship? How do you react to conflict? How does your spouse react to conflict?

- Reflect on your expectations of marriage. Do you think your spouse would consider your expectations realistic? Take time to discuss your expectations with your spouse and discuss your differences.

- What selfish things do you do within your marriage?

- Consider your activities and list any that you put before the Lord and your spouse. Would you consider these things idols?

A Call to Action

- Set aside a few moments during your prayer time to pray for those items that build barriers to oneness in your relationship.

- Think about things you currently do independently that you might need to include your spouse in. These might be financial decisions, decisions about your children, or activities with friends. Work at including your spouse and God in those decisions or activities.

- Pray with your spouse about an area you would like to improve in your marriage.

- When the next big decision/event comes up in your marriage, take time to include God in the process. Pray together, asking for God's direction. He will open or close doors, and He will guide you. Continue to work at this as you grow in your marriage and in your relationship with the Lord.

- Look for activities you can do with your spouse. Coordinate your schedules so you can do them together.

Time with God

- Matthew 19:6: *"So then, they are no longer two but one flesh. Therefore what God has joined together, let not man separate."*

- Genesis 2:24: *"Therefore a man shall leave his father and mother and be joined to his wife, and they shall become one flesh."*

- Ephesians 5:31-33: *"For this reason a man shall leave his father and mother and be joined to his wife, and the two shall become one flesh. . . . Nevertheless let each one of you in particular so love his own wife as himself, and let the wife see that she respects her husband."*

CHAPTER THREE: THE BREASTPLATE

Focus Thought: Protect your heart not only by loving the people around you but also by receiving the love others show to you.

Focus Verse: Beloved, let us love one another, for love is of God; and everyone who loves is born of God and knows God. He who does not love does not know God, for God is love (1 John 4:7-8).

Breastplate of Love

The heart is delicate and an integral part of who we are. It can be crushed by sadness, or it can be filled with joy. The state of your heart determines how you look and act. If you are depressed or sad, your outward appearance will depict a looming cloud. You may come across as unmotivated and ominous. If you are happy and joyful on the inside, your outward appearance will light up and express that joy. Others will likely perceive you as peaceful and confident.

We may try to hide the way we feel inside, but a joyful spirit shines through any countenance like a light. Have you asked yourself how your demeanor comes across to those you meet? Does your expression show misery or does your smile shine the light of Jesus?

Our heart is vulnerable and easily affected by our surroundings and our companions. Because of this vulnerability, you must learn to protect it. If you feel resentment or complacency or you are unable to forgive, you should immediately ask God for wisdom. If you are not sure why you feel that way, ask God, and He will reveal it to you. He will also give you the ability to re-establish feelings of love.

To protect ourselves, we must limit the negativity we expose ourselves to and the level of confrontation we involve ourselves in. Both of these areas will penetrate the breastplate that protects your heart. We must learn to shy away from situations and surroundings that entertain these delinquencies toward love.

Helping your spouse protect their heart is as important as protecting your own. You can do this by showing unconditional love and respect to your spouse. This sounds like common sense; however, most relationships suffer because one spouse feels as if the other has stopped doing it. We need to be conscious of our spouse's needs and discern when they feel vulnerable to love.

You can protect your hearts by committing to remain in love during ALL times and ALL seasons of your marriage. You must communicate how much you love each other no matter what the circumstance. If your spouse struggles with communicating their feelings, remind them of your love periodically so they don't have to worry about it. Fantasize and dream together!

If you're a young married couple, communicating your feelings may be difficult because you're afraid of what the other person may think. You may be insecure about yourself and not want to show any vulnerability to your new spouse. You may find it easy just to say I love you without expressing that you aren't feeling love back.

Communicating your feelings can also be difficult for more seasoned relationships. If you've been in a relationship for a long time, you may feel it won't do any good to repeat how you feel, since nothing has changed since the last time you gained courage to express your feelings. We can get discouraged if we have tried things in the past and have not received the desired result.

We are not all equipped to discuss our feelings easily. Some spouses keep their emotions inside and are not transparent at all. Recognizing problems will require deeper discernment in these relationships. Work at discovering the times when your spouse struggles. They may rely on you to recognize their pain since they have trouble talking about it. Applying the breastplate of love also means spending time looking into your heart to see if anything, anyone, or any thought hinders your love. This daily self-evaluation prevents resentment and other barriers from building up over time.

When you spend time in reflection, make sure you love yourself too. Ask yourself if unworthiness or guilt hinder you from loving yourself. God is merciful and forgiving. As we grow in our relationship with God, we learn to ask Him for forgiveness for our past mistakes. You must be honest with yourself before you can let it go. God's love for you is never-ending, so embrace His love and realize the special person you are.

Finally, you must also receive the love being shown to you. Sometimes we think others show us love in order to get something from us. We need to give and accept love unconditionally. If we struggle to love ourselves, it becomes difficult to receive love. Strong feelings of unworthiness steal our ability to accept love. This will cause tension with your spouse. It may come across to them as anger or disinterest. You must be honest and open with your spouse if you have difficulty accepting their love.

As you learn to apply your marriage armor daily, you'll be able to protect your heart by loving the people around you and receiving the love shown to you. As you go through this process and your relationship with God grows, you will find it much easier to love. Fall in love with your Father, who created you. Grasp the depths of His love. That is a great way to keep your heart protected.

What Motivates Love?

The reason for falling in love varies from marriage to marriage, but we generally fall in love because of an immediate connection either at a physical, intellectual, or spiritual level. As our marriages mature, we can sometimes outgrow and even forget the original reason we fell in love. The pace at which this occurs can vary, depending on the closeness and stability of the relationship.

Because of this possibility, we need to have a good understanding of what motivates our love. What if, before you said "I do," someone told you that you would fall out of love with your spouse within two years? Would you still marry them?

I'm sure you would deny the possibility of falling out of love, even though we've all watched many marriages fall apart because the husband and/or wife supposedly "fell out of love" with the other. Many times the excuse is, "We've grown apart," or "They are not the same person I married." How do we prevent our marriages from falling victim to these excuses? Is there a way to stay in love with the person you marry until the day you die? Is this even something young boys and girls fantasize about anymore? Are we entering into marriage believing we will be with that person forever?

If we do not start our relationship believing it's going to last, we cannot expect it to. At the first sign of trouble, we look for the door and escape the commitment. But if you have started your relationship believing you want to spend the rest of your life with them, then you need to protect the love in your relationship at all costs!

We must learn how to love, and that means attaching no strings to the love we give. Would Jesus put conditions on His love for us? Isn't He the perfect example of love? If we can learn how to love by Jesus' example, we can build a breastplate strong enough to protect our heart and our marriage.

If you find yourself loving only at times when your spouse loves you back, you will encounter many unhappy days. Protecting your heart includes loving yourself and your spouse unconditionally as Jesus loves us, not just when others' actions provoke it. If your marriage is confrontational and neither of you is willing to back down, you are on course for a meltdown. Imagine the same scenario, but this time one spouse is willing to lay aside their pride and show love instead. This will save marriages. Showing love when the other doesn't is selflessness. We all need to work at this. I challenge you to spend time reflecting on your motivation to love. Are you motivated solely by others' actions? Do you respond the same way your spouse responds to you?

Love Yourself

Loving yourself may sound selfish; however, you need to love yourself before you can love others. As it says in Romans 13:9, "For the commandments 'You shall not commit adultery,' 'You shall not murder,' 'You shall not steal,' 'You shall not bear false witness,' 'You shall not covet,' and if there is any other commandment, are all summed up in this saying, namely, 'You shall love your neighbor as yourself.'"

If we are commanded to love our neighbor as ourselves, isn't it important to learn to love ourselves? If we don't have love for ourselves, how can we love our neighbor and fulfill God's commandments? You may think you can love those around you when you are not fully satisfied with yourself. However, I expect you are not being completely honest with yourself. When I suffered depression many times in my marriage, I had a hard time expressing love. I couldn't find joy within myself. Why would I think I could offer someone else what I didn't have?

Each day, we need to spend time reflecting on our hearts and asking God to show us any issues that could hinder us from loving ourselves. You may realize you have some secrets hidden in the deep chamber of your heart, and those secrets have kept you from forgiving and accepting yourself for who you are. If this is the case, you will not be able to give yourself completely in love to someone else.

If you need to find additional strength in this area, read about God's love for you, especially in the Psalms. You'll find joy and strength in understanding the depths of God's love for us. As you and your spouse continue to deepen your relationship with God, you will find it easier to love. God requires us to love others and to receive love from Him. Spend time falling in love with God so you can find ways to love yourself.

Loving your Spouse

Loving your spouse is paramount to ensuring that your marriage will last. It's not enough to know you love them; you must also show your love. Embracing your spouse's imperfections will protect their heart and yours too. We all have areas that need improvement, so do not base your love for your spouse on a point system or a task-completed system.

If you entered your relationship thinking you would change the person you married, making them everything you need, you will probably never give the love that your spouse needs. You will always be waiting for them to measure up to the standard in your mind. As couples, we need to learn to love each other unconditionally. This goes hand-in-hand with the expectations we set for our relationship. When you learn to love your spouse unconditionally, their faults will not cause you to waiver in that love.

Imagine someone saying they will love you if you complete A, B, C, and D steps. Would you consider that love to be sincere? No, so why do we secretly keep this grading scale in the depths of our minds and hearts when it comes to our spouses? A love-filled household is also crucial to raising healthy children. If you have children and they do not see love between you and your spouse, how will they learn to love? You must set the example! Our children learn to love or hate, forgive or resent by watching us as parents and adults. In fact, our actions in the home affect how our children interact with their friends and enemies and how they will treat their future spouse.

Demonstrating love to your spouse in front of your children will protect them. Don't be afraid to show small signs of affection when they are around. A kiss, a hug, even a smile between a husband and wife are great ways to raise children with love in their hearts.

You can find endless ways to express love to your spouse. Be creative and make sure you never stop! Send packages to their work filled with goodies that will remind them of a happy memory of time you spent together. Leave a love note on the hood of their car. Leave a message on the bathroom mirror. These are fun ways to demonstrate love. Find out what your spouse responds to and feed into those areas.

Protecting your heart and your spouse's heart will bring joy to your life. Coldly saying, "I love you" is not convincing to most people. Actions mean much more than words. I challenge you to find new ways to let your spouse know you love them.

Loving Others

Loving others will strengthen the breastplate of love, which will ultimately protect your marriage. Try to love others more than you've ever loved them before. From your neighbor who has lived next door to you for the past two years to the woman you pass at the grocery store, show love! By looking beyond ourselves and toward the needs of others, you open your heart to love, and it becomes more sensitive. You will find joy in loving others and seeing them sense your love. Sharing a smile with the unknown person in the grocery line will lighten their day and will, in turn, make you smile.

Giving love to others, and seeing them receive it, will build the bond between you and your spouse. As you reach out to others affectionately, you and your spouse will draw closer than ever before. You create unity in your relationship as you learn to combine efforts in loving others.

Maybe one of you is stronger at this than the other. If so, don't be discouraged. As you set the example, your spouse will see your efforts. They will eventually come around because they will see how showing love changes your life and your outlook. Don't be afraid or discouraged to be the example. Before long, your spouse will step up.

Interestingly, the Bible tells us to avoid debt other than the debt of love. Romans 13:8 says, *"Owe no one anything except to love one another, for he who loves another has fulfilled the law."* This shows that loving others is not only satisfying but is also required of us. And not only is it required of us, but we should feel indebted to love. Imagine how the world would be if we loved even those we never meet. Consider spending time in prayer for the homeless, our children, our military, and our nation. This is the kind of love we should feel indebted to.

When you see someone in need, remember that you are indebted to helping them, even if it's just with a smile. I've often passed someone and recognized they were in a bad place or felt alone. Making eye contact and offering a smile during those times seems small, but at times, I have felt it has had great impact. If you feel led to shake someone's hand or to say a word of encouragement, don't hesitate. This is usually God nudging you to be His hands and mouth and to give a hug in His name.

Don't miss the opportunity to turn someone's day from bad to something better. No act of kindness is too small. Love is a gift that cannot be packaged or priced. It is limitless and we have enough to give freely. As a couple, encourage each other to love those around you and those you haven't met. Don't judge, gossip, or criticize. If one of you starts down that path of negativity, your partner must stand up and hold them accountable.

We cannot say we love others as God loves us if we ridicule them. Learning to love is crucial to keeping the right spirit and protecting your heart. The sense of humility you will develop will directly affect your marriage. Respect will build as you and your spouse grow in love. We should encourage our spouses to develop this priceless trait at all cost.

If anyone boasts, "I love God," and goes right on hating his brother or sister, thinking nothing of it, he is a liar. If he won't love the person he can see, how can he love the God he can't see? The command we have from Christ is blunt: Loving God includes loving people. You've got to love both. (1 John 4:20-21)

Receiving Love

Receiving love can be as important as showing love. We must receive love in a marriage in order to maintain a strong bond. This can be difficult at times. You may resist your spouse's love out of stubbornness, and it can cause further separation during a time of conflict. When your spouse shows you love, especially after an argument, make sure you accept it. Don't question the love they are trying to show you.

If you struggle with accepting love, it might be because of a trust issue or because you do not love yourself. You need then to ask God again to open your eyes to the reason you cannot receive love unconditionally. You may have been hurt in the past, and that may cloud your ability to believe someone can love you for who you are.

If you struggle with receiving love, you may also need to spend time recognizing the love God has for you. His love for you is so deep, it should be peaceful to the heart. Be protected, knowing His love never fails! As a couple, work on trusting God's love by thanking him for the mercy and grace He gives you each day.

Barriers to Love

There is a variety of reasons why we either choose not to love or choose not to receive love. These barriers include, resentment, unforgiveness, and fear. Any combination can be deadly and have significant effects on our heart. We must be able to identify what barriers hinder our ability to love or receive love. Most importantly, we should be honest with ourselves and hold ourselves accountable.

Resentment: Resentment will destroy any relationship! At all costs, resolve all resentment you may have hidden in your heart. If you resist praying for someone, even your spouse, you have probably built up resentment or hate.

I remember once having trouble praying for someone I knew needed it. Every time I tried to pray for them, a black wall would appear in my mind. I got distracted then frustrated and eventually gave up trying to pray. God soon showed me that I needed to deal with my unresolved resentment toward this person before I could progress in prayer. I had to come to terms with why I resented them, and I had to ask God for forgiveness.

I can now close my eyes and pray for this person. What a victory! What a selfless gift to give your enemy: time in the prayer room, asking God to protect them, bless them, and guide them. I would have disappointed myself if I hadn't been able to overcome this barrier. Be encouraged to keep pressing through.

Unforgiveness: Unforgiveness is a lot like resentment in the sense that it can destroy any relationship. Unforgiveness will cause a huge dent in the breastplate that protects your heart. We hold onto unforgiveness for many reasons. It can grow for years and years in your heart. Be careful if you feel any unforgiveness toward your spouse. As soon as you sense it, you must resolve it. Too many times, we get hurt and hold onto the pain for years. Eventually, your love will be strained to a point of no return. Learn to forgive each other at all cost.

Don't end any conversation without forgiving. When my husband and I have a disagreement or trust issue, we discuss it. At times I may need to give him a few minutes alone first, but we eventually come together to resolve it and put it behind us. Be careful with all unforgiveness because you never know if something will happen to you or your spouse. Don't put yourself in a posture of regret. Learn to love each other unconditionally!

Learning to Forgive: A Personal Story

During various times in my marriage my husband has chosen his addition over our love. The addiction has driven him to places of deceit, theft, and dishonor. When we went through times when he has chosen to give up everything for one high, it can be very difficult to forgive. Often, we feel like our spouse must not love us because they were able to hurt us. As someone who is not an addict, I get confused and extremely hurt when I experience this destructive behavior. I have found that I have held resentment in my heart toward him because of what he has put us through. He could also feel this resentment long after we restored our marriage. I had to confront forgiveness, and so did he. In order for our marriage to move forward, not only did I have to forgive him, but he had to forgive himself for the destruction and pain he caused.

The longer he goes not forgiving himself, the more of a possibility he will fall again. When things started going good, he would feel unworthy of good things because of his past mistakes, so he would fall again. Only by the grace of God have we overcome these pains, been able to forgive, and move forward. This has remained a daily commitment in our marriage. If memories resurface, I call on the name of Jesus, and He remains my comfort and my shield. Allow God to work in your life, and you will be able to overcome anything!

Fear: Fear will suffocate most joyful things in life, especially love. You might fear what may happen, what others think about you, or that your spouse doesn't love you. This focus on fear will consume you and hinder your growth. It will cause you to deny love and can tear apart

57

any relationship. Fear has caused many issues in my marriage and in my walk with God. I have allowed fear to consume me rather than walking in faith.

Realizing that God has your life in His hands. No matter what happens, He will make a way for you. When I feel worry coming on, I immediately begin saying, "I trust You, God." Doing this provides comfort to my spirit and allows the fear to subside. Don't let fear win. We cannot control what is going to happen, so we must remember WHO is in control. Fear must not be allowed in your marriage.

Love is Accountable

Finally, to ensure the breastplate of love is fully formed and impenetrable, we must have accountability. Being accountable for our actions doesn't mean a whole lot when we tell people we love them but talk them down when they are absent. It also doesn't mean a whole lot when we tell our spouse we love them and then hold resentment in our heart. There must be accountability as you give and receive love.

God will always know your true feelings and actions, but it is a great day when we can hold ourselves accountable to our spouse. Take time together to reflect on how you treat others. Spend time discussing how you feel your spouse has been treating you. Both of you need to be open to accepting and receiving criticism.

The final step is to spend time in prayer, confiding in God about your problem areas. If you are having a hard time forgiving someone, make sure to tell God. Also, ask God from time to time to show you things that could build barriers to your ability to love or receive love. Accountability is crucial in all we do.

On our final day, when the Book of Life is opened in heaven, we will be held accountable for what we've done with our lives. Imagine God turning to the first page under your name. The page is filled with various words partially down the page. You ask "What do those words say?"

God responds, "These are your evil, hurtful actions."

He turns to the next page. It too is filled with writing, but this time the writing goes further down the page. You ask again, "What do those words say?" God says, "Those are the evil, hurtful words you spoke throughout your life."

Yet again, as you nervously stand by, God flips the page. It is full of words. Afraid to ask, but unable to hold back, you ask again, "What do these words say?" "These are all the evil thoughts you had during your life."

At this point, you are frozen in fear, for there is yet another page. The next and final page is so filled with ink, it almost looks black. Since you are unable to ask what those words represent, God discloses, "These are the evil and resentful things that resided in your heart."

As you can tell by this illustration, your heart clearly defines who you are. Though we rarely act out all our thoughts and the secrets of our hearts, it is the uncleanness of the heart that we must hold ourselves accountable to. We may look polished on the outside, but the heart projects our true intentions.

To love and be loved, we must pray for a clean heart. As we ask God to reveal what is in our hearts, and as we begin to correct what He reveals, our thoughts, words, and actions will surely follow.

Gird your Breastplate

The breastplate of love, when applied correctly, will protect your heart completely. It's not enough, however, just to apply the breastplate loosely. You must bind it, strap it, support it, and fortify it. Love cannot be taken lightly, and we must learn all facets of it. Take the time to love others, learn to love yourself, and make sure your love for your spouse and for God is always on fire!

If you find your heart exposed to the vulnerability of attacks, implement the changes necessary in order to tighten up your breastplate of love. Never let your heart be hardened! Instead, develop a sincere and receptive heart that is softened to hear great things.

Too often, we hear that love is not enough to cause a marriage to survive. This downplays the power of love. I want you to hold onto the greatest gift God gives as stated in 1 Corinthians 13:4-8a: "Love suffers long and is kind; love does not envy; love does not parade itself, is not puffed up; does not behave rudely, does not seek its own, is not provoked, thinks no evil; does not rejoice in iniquity, but rejoices in the truth; bears all things, believes all things, hopes all things, endures all things. Love never fails. . . ."

Believing in love means you will always have hope, you can always endure, and your love will not fail. How awesome that, as a couple, you can know that if you protect the love between you, your gift is a hope beyond hope. Take time each day to be ready to love your spouse, receive love from your spouse, love others, and hope and dream together.

TIME TO ENGAGE

You must apply the breastplate of love each day in order to protect your heart. A hardened heart will damage your marriage. As you grow closer to God, your heart will become softer and more receptive. Let yourself be vulnerable to the work God wants to do in your life. Learn to love yourself, love others, receive love, and be accountable to love. Don't let love be a burden; instead, let it fill you with joy!

Questions for Reflection

- What can you do to concentrate on loving your spouse? What barriers hinder you from showing love to your spouse even when you know they could use your encouragement?

- List different ways you can show love to your spouse. What fun things can you do to accomplish this? (Memory box delivered to work, love note on car, secret weekend away, or a framed photograph of a memory you share.)

- Reflect on ways to show love to others. This could be toward people at work, people at church, and strangers.

- Take a look inside your heart and ask these questions: Do I harbor resentment toward my spouse? Are there areas I need to forgive?

- How can your spouse hold you accountable for love? Think of areas you struggle in, whether it is receiving love, loving your spouse, or loving others. How can your spouse help you?

A Call to Action

- Write a list of things you love about your spouse. Find a moment to share these with your spouse.

- Set aside time to practice changing your focus from your feelings to your spouse's feelings. Make a commitment to love your spouse daily by focusing on their needs.

- List four things you can do to increase physical affection in your marriage. Take time each week to implement these changes. Start doing them today!

- Think of ways you can create an atmosphere of love or closeness. Each week, schedule one of these with your spouse. It is important to keep the love alive in your marriage. You must continue to have quality time alone.

Time with God

- 1 Thessalonians 3:12-13: *"And may the Lord make you increase and abound in love to one another and to all, just as we do to you, so that He may establish your hearts blameless in holiness before our God. . . ."*

- Romans 15:1-2: *"We then who are strong ought to bear with the scruples of the weak, and not to please ourselves. Let each of us please his neighbor for his good, leading to edification."*

- Ephesians 4:2: *"With all lowliness and gentleness, with longsuffering, bearing with one another in love . . ."*

- Luke 6:35: *"But love your enemies, do good, and lend, hoping for nothing in return; and your reward will be great, and you will be sons of the Most High."*

- Romans 5:8: *"But God demonstrates His own love toward us, in that while we were still sinners, Christ died for us."*

CHAPTER FOUR: SHOES

Focus Thought: Have the heart of a servant and wash your loved one's feet.

Focus Verse: Work with enthusiasm, as though you were working for the Lord rather than for people (Ephesians 6:7, NLT).

Shoes of Servitude

What does it mean to have a servant's heart or to walk in a servant's shoes? Jesus is the perfect example of this type of servant. He showed loved without condition and did selfless acts for everyone he met. A true servant works hard to meet the needs of those they serve. They serve without question and with humility.

A perfect example of this type of servitude is when Jesus washed His apostles' feet. Though He was clearly their leader, He chose to be a servant to His followers. He showed that the best leaders are those who humble themselves and serve.

As husband and wife, we must apply the shoes of servitude as a part of our daily routine. Marriage is a give-and-take affair, but sometimes we may feel as if we give more than we take. This can cause resentment or frustration. During these times, we need to remember the example Jesus demonstrated for us.

It is not uncommon to enjoy being served rather than to serve. Not having to work for something is appealing, and most of us would rather have it that way. However, a selfless attitude and trying to please the other will have a positive effect on your marriage. Selflessness will go miles when you put your spouse before yourself. Putting others first is a way of demonstrating love from the most humble state. It will bring peace in your household, because love will not allow any room for resentment. As we read in Philippians 2:3: *"Let nothing be done through selfish ambition or conceit, but in lowliness of mind let each esteem others better than himself."*

When you learn to be selfless, you learn to esteem others. Making others feel good, especially your spouse, is generosity without a price tag. Love in marriage goes hand in hand with selflessness. Being selfless in your actions and words is not always easy. Now, I'm pretty sure that everyone reading this is just like me and has *never been* selfish and *always* put others before you.

Okay, so that's not true! We are human, and it's natural for us all to be selfish and to want others to do things for us. Personally, I struggle daily to put others before myself. I would rather have someone help me with my need or cater to my desires.

When you have this type of thought, try taking some time to think about the following points. If you do, it may be easier to put your spouse's needs before your own.

- How many times are you supposed to be patient and kind when your spouse keeps doing the same annoying thing over and over again? Are you normally on the giving or receiving end of this type of behavior? Do you do anything that annoys your spouse? Why do you continue to do them?

- How do you keep from being irritable when you have had the worst day ever, and your head is pounding? Has your spouse ever overreacted toward you because they had a bad day or they weren't feeling well? How did it make you feel?

- Do you have expectations of life, marriage, and one another? Are you impatient when those expectations are not met? Does your spouse have expectations of you that you aren't able to meet?

Part of our commitment to marriage includes a level of selflessness that must be incorporated into each day. Since our natural tendency is to let others serve us, it's important that we remember to apply the shoes of service daily. Consider Jesus' example and challenge yourself each day to lay down the selfish desires you hold onto.

Selfishness will drive people away, especially your spouse. No matter how strong your relationship becomes, you must always keep your selfish nature under control. As soon as you allow it to surface and you begin to exhibit selfish behaviors, you will poison your relationship.

Finally, are you asking the right questions about your marriage? The wrong questions are: "If I do this, will it make her want to divorce me?" and "How much can I get away with and still stay married?" If you ask these questions, you are doing the minimum to keep your relationship intact. A better question would be, "What can I do today to please my wife?" or "What would make my husband's day today a little easier?"

These types of questions are asked out of love and a desire to please your spouse. Can you see the difference between the two examples? How do you think these relationships will differ? One household will enjoy love and respect; whereas, the other will be filled with competition, deceit, and selfishness. Do you ask the right questions?

Sacrifice

Many of us are either unable or unwilling to have a servant's heart consistently. I have difficulty with this, because I, too, have legitimate needs. The ability to look past your own needs, give them up, and serve the other is priceless in a marriage.

You may think this is easier said than done. True, but isn't that what sacrifice is all about? Overlooking your own needs is a huge sacrifice, and it isn't easy. There is a way to approach each day humbly and with the mindset of serving the one you love. Each morning, take time to give God your needs and burdens. This will release you from those weights so you can serve those around you. Spend time each day reflecting on what you can do for your spouse. As you learn to give your burdens and needs to God while focusing on your spouse's needs, you'll find great satisfaction.

Serve those around you out of love. If you serve your spouse or others because you were told to, it will seem like work. Sacrifice, when done from the heart, will bring joy to each step. Let serving become a passion that sparks new interest each day. The more you learn to give of yourself, the more you'll receive in return. In time, as you give more and more to your spouse in love, you will notice the love returned.

Submission

To submit is to yield or to subject oneself to another. If we are submissive, we are humble or compliant. Serving requires submission. It may mean we submit our pride or that we take direction from our spouse. Submission can be a scary word in today's society, and we sometimes conceive it as weakness. Biblically, God wants us to submit to Him and the authority He places in our lives. As a husband and wife, read this passage:

> *Wives, submit to your own husbands, as to the Lord. For the husband is head of the wife, as also Christ is head of the church; and He is the Savior of the body. Therefore, just as the church is subject to Christ, so let the wives be to their own husbands in everything. Husbands, love your wives, just as Christ also loved the church and gave Himself for her, that He might sanctify and*

70

cleanse her with the washing of water by the word, that He

might present her to Himself a glorious church, not having spot

or wrinkle, but that she should be holy and without blemish. So

husbands ought to love their own wives as their own bodies; he

who loves his wife loves himself. (Ephesians 5:22-28)

Submission, as detailed here, is a two-way street. Not only does the wife submit to her husband, but the husband is required to submit to God's authority. In addition, the husband must show respect and love to his wife. All too often, the term submission is taken out of context and can seem one-sided. It is important, in order to wear the shoes of a servant, that both husband and wife know how to submit.

As men draw closer to God, they develop integrity, humility, and servitude. Wives, encourage your husband to build his relationship with God. Being the head of the household is a daunting task and is not one that should be taken lightly.

As women draw closer to God, they develop patience, love, and humility. Husbands, encourage your wives to build their relationship with God. Learning to submit to a husband is difficult for a lot of women and can seem old-fashioned in today's society.

Husbands, you must love your wife and encourage her inner beauty. Together, as you learn submission, order will fall into place within your household. Roles will naturally define, and you'll have security and peace in the home. Submission cannot work if it is one-sided. Husbands and wives must work together in clearly defined roles established by God.

Show Interest

What could be more flattering than having your spouse show interest in whatever you are doing? You may think you do that already, but are you doing it with the right spirit? Do you keep your spouse's well-being in the forefront as you show interest? It is important, as you walk in a servant's shoes, that you encourage your spouse to develop. Showing interest will make them feel loved and connected.

How you show interest in your spouse depends on your spouse and how they like to be shown love. My husband needs me to show interest in his music. He is very passionate about his music. It brings a lot of joy to him if I'm actively involved in helping him achieve his musical goals or even to be a sounding board for his ideas. Find what your spouse is passionate about and dive into it with them.

Replace Your Worn-out Shoes and Keep Serving

As your relationships progress, grow, and mature, you may spend less and less time applying your shoes of servitude. Maybe your shoes don't fit anymore or they are too worn out to wear.

As you and your spouse mature, your needs will change. What you do today to serve your spouse may not be what your spouse will desire five years down the road. You'll want to recognize when you have grown out of your shoes and when you must to replace them. We must keep the servant attitude fresh, never letting service to others grow old or become a chore. Never forget the reward you receive when you serve others. Your marriage's health depends on it.

TIME TO ENGAGE

The Shoes of Service, when applied each day, allow us to see the needs of those around us. Consciously making a decision to serve your spouse and those around you, even when your needs are not being met, takes strength only God can provide. Start each day asking God for the heart of a servant. Ask for strength and humility to meet the needs of those around you. As you learn to trust God, you'll find He is there to meet all your needs.

Questions for Reflection

- Reflect on your spouse's needs and the things they like to do. How can you help them with those needs?

- What happens when you don't get your way? How can you work at changing how you react?

- How does your spouse behave under the same circumstances? What do you do when they don't get their way and react negatively?

- Wives, can you submit to your husband as detailed in

Ephesians 5? Husbands, can you submit to God and love your wife as yourself? Order in the household is important to a healthy marriage. Spend time understanding your role.

- What are some ways you can show interest in your spouse? Do you need to be the center of attention? If so, how can you shift interest from yourself to your spouse?

A Call to Action

- At the start of each week, make a list of things you can do for your spouse. Work at accomplishing at least one thing a day that forces you to be selfless.

- As a couple, do something for your neighbor as an act of kindness. Ask for nothing in return.

- Work at fasting at least once a month as a way to discipline yourself to sacrifice. You can fast some type of food you love, caffeine, Internet, or television.

- What does your spouse do that you can show interest in? Come up with concrete ways you can let your spouse know you are interested in them.

Time with God

- I Peter 3:1-5, 7: *"Wives, likewise, be submissive to your own husbands, that even if some do not obey the word, they, without a word, may be won by the conduct of their wives, when they observe your chaste conduct accompanied by fear. Do not let your adornment be merely outward— arranging the hair, wearing gold, or putting on fine apparel— rather let it be the hidden person of the heart, with the incorruptible beauty of a gentle and quiet spirit, which is very precious in the sight of God. For in this manner, in former times, the holy women who trusted in God also adorned themselves, being submissive to their own husbands . . . Husbands, likewise, dwell with them with understanding, giving honor to the wife, as to the weaker vessel, and as being heirs together of the grace of life, that your prayers may not be hindered."*

- Philippians 2:3: *"Let nothing be done through selfish ambition or conceit, but in lowliness of mind let each esteem others better than himself."*

- Proverbs 15:1: *"A soft answer turns away wrath, but a harsh word stirs up anger."*

CHAPTER FIVE: THE SHIELD

Focus Thought: Connect in prayer and God will shield you from danger.

Focus Verse: Behold, I stand at the door and knock. If anyone hears My voice and opens the door, I will come in to him and dine with him, and he with Me (Revelation 3:20).

Shield of Prayer

We all want our families safe and protected. But do we pray daily for it? Praying for a hedge of protection around your family will shield you from danger. This is especially true for military families. We sometimes have difficulty believing that God wants to hear our prayers and keep us safe. This doubt can inhibit the faith necessary for effective prayer. We must believe and trust that God hears our prayers and knows what is best for us. We must pray diligently about everything that concerns us.

We need several levels of disciplined prayer. First, we should make time for quiet, one-on-one prayer time. At other times, we need loud, forthright prayer to conduct spiritual warfare and win battles.

Prayer together with your spouse is also powerful, although many couples struggle to pray together.

Connecting spiritually will keep your marriage strong. Work together by sharing scripture, claiming victories in your lives, and praying for God's will for your family and protection for your children. All these types of prayer will build an impenetrable shield of protection around your family.

Become faithful in prayer if you haven't had that type of walk with God yet. Deciding to commit to prayer every day is a discipline we must work at. Prayer may require a sacrifice of time and sleep. It requires you to clear your mind, to forgive others, to forgive yourself, and to look into your heart for other imperfections.

Once you build your prayer life, you and your spouse can be an unbeatable team. Learn how to be an example to your children by incorporating prayer into their lives. This priceless gift can never be taken away from them.

Finally, don't be intimated by prayer. Often we think only the church leaders can pray. We may believe we have to know Bible verse after Bible verse and appropriate language in order to come before

God. This is not true. God wants to be our friend. He desires to hear from us! We need to learn to talk to God as we would talk to a friend.

What a missed opportunity when God waits patiently for you, but you don't take the time to talk to Him. He wants you to come and meet with Him. Don't leave Him standing at the door too long. Develop a desire to chat with the best friend you could ever have.

Time Alone with God

The shield of prayer will protect your family from anything that comes against it. Beginning each day in private prayer time is the key to strengthening that shield. Our personal time connecting with God requires self-discipline, but the rewards are much greater than the small sacrifice of time. Getting on my knees and spending time with my Creator is easier some days than others. At times, I want to talk to God but yet have nothing to say. Other times I anxiously wait to hear from God about the direction of my life, but He seems far away.

Do you have days like this? God's desire during those times is for us to keep pushing through until we hear from Him. Those are the times He requires patience from us. How often do we find ourselves giving up before God has the chance to bless us? I'm sure I've missed many awesome moves of God because of my own agenda.

We all experience those moments. Our minds can get so consumed by the thoughts of the day that we can't hear Him whisper. When your mind is hard to quiet, imagine the large bowls kept in heaven that hold the prayers of God's righteous people. Visualize your prayers falling into these bowls. God is waiting for the day these bowls of prayer spill over from the cries of His people. Be persistent when you become distracted, and push forward.

You can also take a structured prayer journey that is designed to make it easier for you to focus:

- *Praise/Worship:* This step includes recognizing God for His glory and thanking Him for the air you breathe. Think of it as welcoming Him into your presence. Invite Him!

- *Repentance/Forgiveness:* Look deep into your heart at those barriers we discussed earlier. Ask God to reveal any areas of unforgiveness or resentment. Ask for forgiveness of your sins.

- *Petition:* When you petition God, you are asking Him for things you desire. These desires shouldn't necessarily mean a new car or other "want." Petition Him for your needs and hopes and dreams. Be specific and place all your cares and worries into His hands.

- *Intercession:* When you intercede, you are praying for others. You may develop a long list of intercessory needs. Intercede on behalf of others, both people you know and do not know. Your prayer may be what God is waiting for. Never underestimate the power your prayer can have on someone else.

- *Thanksgiving:* Give God thanks and praise in as many ways as you can think of. Be specific or be general in your thanks. Take the time you need to show how grateful you are for the things He has done for you and the things He will yet do. Claim things by giving thanks although the prayer hasn't yet been answered. "Thank you, Jesus, for sending my husband home soon!"

- *Meditation:* During meditation, be quiet and wait to hear a word from the Lord. He may not shout at you, but He may lay a scripture or song on your heart. Be still and wait!

- *Praying the Word:* At this point, use God's word to pray for all other needs. God's word is all-powerful. Learn how to use it to make things happen.

- *Singing:* End your prayer journey with music, whether you hum, whistle, or sing. Show him praise through singing and worship.

If you find it hard to focus on certain days, try to keep the prayer journey steps nearby. I find it helpful to keep my prayer journey steps inside my Bible. This way, if I find myself at a loss for words, I can glance at the journey steps and get back on track.

Time Together with God

Praying with your spouse is beneficial to a marriage. The shield protecting your marriage will be indestructible when combined with the shield of the one you love. Take a moment to close your eyes and imagine yourself holding a shield. Now imagine holding hands with your spouse and with both your shields held together in front of you. Seems impenetrable, doesn't it?

I encourage you to work toward praying as a couple. Many couples resist praying together because they don't know how to do it. It may feel uncomfortable at first. Keep at it! Take time to decide how you would like to structure your prayer time together. For example, will you pray out loud? Will one take the lead? Will you start with praise and move on to needs? Once you become disciplined at praying as a couple, it will feel natural.

You still need time alone with just you and God, but try to spend at least a few minutes with your spouse, praying together for the good of your family. An indescribable closeness comes with quality prayer time with your spouse. Personally, when I see my husband praying and showing a vulnerable side, I find it attractive. It's comforting to know that your husband trusts in the protection and direction God can provide the family. Also, going to church, sharing worship and sharing ministry, and spending quiet prayer times together are encouraging.

In addition to the spiritual closeness, you'll have the benefit of physical closeness. There's a lot of touching when my husband and I pray together, whether we hold hands or have a hand on the other's back. Sometimes you don't realize you've gone a whole day without each other's physical touch. This moment of holding hands gives us a needed connection. It can become a level of intimacy that most couples don't know is available to them. Connecting with your spouse in prayer is one of the most satisfying experiences you will ever feel in your life. Learn to grow and pray together.

Sharing Ministry

One final way to connect in prayer is through ministry. Even if you're not active in church, you may still have a ministry. Possibly you're serving the homeless in your community, working with abused wives and their children, or acting as a big brother or big sister to local youth. Working in ministry is a great way to demonstrate your faith. Anointing of that ministry is done by fervent prayer and constant communication with God to confirm His will.

Ministry can strengthen a marriage by creating a common goal between husband and wife. If you connect in ministry, you will spend constructive time together, planning and setting goals. A passion is developed that you can both foster. Don't be discouraged, however, if you don't share a ministry. Not all husbands and wives have the same passions. What you can do is make sure to support and encourage your spouse, show interest in their ministry, and be a part of it as much as you can.

Sharing Ministry: A Personal Story

My husband and I have always had a passion for ministry. Like most couples, we both had very separate ministries we felt called to lead. Interestingly enough, it wasn't until we were rebuilding our marriage that we were called to our first combined ministry. Our church needed new college and career leaders. I was hesitant about accepting the Pastor's request to head up this ministry, but I was obedient. Not only has this new ministry been personally rewarding, but it has brought my husband and me closer than we've ever been before. Having a combined goal of mentoring this group of young adults has allowed us to share many victories and milestones. We plan together, write classes together, host events together, and pray with and for this group together. Working in this ministry as a team has created a bond between us that continues to strengthen us as a couple.

Pick up Your Shield

Prayer is not going to happen unless you discipline yourself to do it. Finding a prayer life can be difficult and may require you to step out of your comfort zone or put down bad habits. We must evaluate our days and what we designate as priority in our schedules. Once you learn to pick up the shield of prayer daily, protection WILL follow.

The shield of prayer is important in marriage because there is power behind prayer. When we pray, God intervenes on our behalf. As we learn to pray alone and with our spouse, we will develop a long-lasting relationship with the King of kings. Connecting with your spouse in prayer is not only powerful but intimate. Your relationship will bloom beyond imagination when you pick up your shield each day.

Questions for Reflection

- Do you and your spouse currently spend time praying together? If not, are you interested in doing it?

- How consistent is your prayer routine? What can you do to improve it? What would you say is the biggest obstacle to finding time to pray?

- Do you and your spouse share a ministry together? If so, describe the connection you gain from that. If not, would you consider sharing some type of ministry with your spouse?

A Call to Action

- Set up a time of day for private prayer and a time to pray with your spouse. Make a commitment to keep your appointments!

- Develop an area in your home that you will claim as your "prayer closet." Let this be your special place where you communicate with God. Read Matthew 6:6: "But you, when you pray, go into your room, and when you have shut your door, pray to your Father who is in the secret place; and your Father who sees in secret will reward you openly."

- Consider the ministry ideas you came up with. If you aren't currently in ministry together, work at getting your spouse to commit to the idea of doing something together.

- Write down the prayer journey as described in the section "Alone with God." Keep the prayer journey in the area where you pray.

- Commit as a couple to pray for our nation, its leaders, our military and their families, schools, and our children. Work at making this an integral part of your prayer journey.

Time with God

- Hebrews 11:1-3: *"Now faith is the substance of things hoped for, the evidence of things not seen. For by it the elders obtained a good testimony. By faith we understand that the worlds were framed by the word of God, so that the things which are seen were not made of things which are visible."*

- 1 Peter 5:6-7: *"Therefore humble yourselves under the mighty hand of God, that He may exalt you in due time, casting all your care upon Him, for He cares for you."*

- Matthew 18:19-20: *"Again I say to you that if two of you agree on earth concerning anything that they ask, it will be done for them by My Father in heaven. For where two or three are gathered together in My name, I am there in the midst of them."*

CHAPTER SIX: THE HELMET

Focus Thought: Communicating and understanding what the other is thinking will help protect your mind from thoughts of doubt and fear.

Focus Verse: For there is nothing hidden which will not be revealed, nor has anything been kept secret but that it should come to light (Mark 4:22).

———————————●———————————

Helmet of Communication

Communicating with your spouse and family requires daily effort, but the rewards of keeping open lines of communication are priceless. This will protect your family from unneeded arguments. Be open and effective in your desire to communicate.

This means there should be no secrets or lies in a marriage. All too often, we fail to equate holding back part of the story with lying. Deceit and lies are easy to sense. They make the victim uneasy. Protect your relationship by keeping honesty and truth in your communication. Knowing what your spouse is thinking will protect you from doubts and fear. Any sign of deceit in your spouse can cause tremendous fear, worry, and anxiety. Those unknowns or possibilities will take over and control your thoughts and emotions and can destroy a marriage.

The helmet of communication will protect your mind. As with the other pieces of armor, you must apply the helmet each day. When we allow ourselves to entertain discouraging or fearful thoughts, we become vulnerable to unneeded attacks. When we allow our minds to wander, our actions, our words, and our demeanor are all affected.

Barriers to Communication

Communication in marriage is critical, yet many barriers can affect how well we do it. Some of these barriers include:

- Technology

- Schedules

- Pride

- Thoughts (negativity, resentment, worthlessness, fear)

- Deceit

- Lack of focus

You need to understand how each of the barriers can impact your communication with your spouse, with God, with your friends, and with your family. We must not take these barriers lightly.

Technology: Technology is a wonderful yet destructive innovation. Generation after generation has seen technology advance at astounding rates. Today, technological advancements allow us to communicate more effectively and more often. Unfortunately, technology's downside eats away at our families, stealing valuable family time we used to enjoy. Many of us eat dinner in front of the television, text at the table, or eat while working on the computer. Quality time that husbands and wives used to share has now turned into time on the computer. Networking sites now meet socialization needs that our marriages used to fill.

You can find multiple computers in homes these days, with husbands and wives on separate computers doing separate things. We can get Internet access anywhere, thanks to iPhones, iPads and other devices. We can surf the Internet while sitting on the couch, watching television. Mobster and vampire-type games take the place of reading God's word together.

Pornography is also readily available now because of the Internet and pay-per-view adult channels. If you allow pornography into your home, it will poison your relationship. Pornography is an addiction, and viewing it will only make it worse. Take the time to install pornography blockers on devices that provide access to it.

So has technology helped or hindered communication? I suppose the answer is both. Each household must learn to balance the use of technology in the home. Set boundaries for usage for the entire family. Don't let technology run rampant in your home. Agree as husband and wife to set those boundaries, and enforce them by holding each other accountable.

Schedules: Schedules today are overwhelmingly busy. Families run from work to the gym to kids' sporting events, church, dance class, and more. If you schedule every hour of your day with activities, when will you have time to share quality moments with your spouse? You need some down time so you can have conversation, intimacy, and affection. If you run here and there every night of the week and all weekend, you will drift apart. Your life will revolve only around getting tasks done versus enjoying life. We must have balance!

Pride: Pride is a barrier to communication. If you allow pride to rise up when you are talking with your spouse, you probably won't hear what they have to say. Self-love and pride can cause you to tune out what others have to say. How can your spouse feel like an equal partner if this is going on? When one spouse is prideful, it can cause resentment in the other spouse. It may cause them to lose self-esteem and feel worthless when the other is always boasting about being right. We must learn to treat each other with respect and not allow pride to rise up when we communicate. Also, be careful that you don't allow pride to force submission from your spouse. Submission is done out of love and respect.

Thoughts: Thoughts of negativity, resentment, worthlessness, and fear are all barriers to communication. Often, these emotions scatter our thoughts. They might cause you to pull back in conversations and prevent you from wanting to communicate. They can lead to depression, which will have severe effects on a marriage.

Entertaining these types of thoughts will bring anyone down and cause them to withdraw. We must learn to dwell on positive thoughts and thoughts about God's promises. Train your mind to transform situations into opportunities rather than obstacles. Training your mind to do this will make you less likely to fear or think negatively about the situation. Your thoughts are powerful in determining your demeanor and actions.

Deceit: Deceit and manipulation bring dishonesty and trust issues into a marriage. Honesty in our relationships will help to keep our marriages healthy. The best thing you can do for your spouse is to be honest about every situation, not alter the facts, and not lie by omission.

If a couple is honest, they can work through most trials and regain trust. However, lost trust is hard to earn back. Also, if one spouse feels as if the other manipulates them all the time, they are less likely to open up or give insight. This person feels backed into a corner or pressured.

How can you have effective communication in your marriage when you feel this? Be careful to look at how you communicate with your spouse. Don't allow yourself to be deceitful or manipulative, because it could destroy all trust in your relationship.

Lack of focus: Lack of focus causes barriers in communication, especially if you are both off doing your own thing and not focusing on the family needs. Is your household like this? Do you lack focus as a couple? You may be very driven independently, but if the two of you don't share similar goals, you run the risk of growing apart. If you have lost interest in your marriage, you will have a hard time focusing. Also, if there is always confrontation when you communicate, you won't have effective results.

Spend time in reflection and ask yourself whether you initiate any of those barriers that hinder your relationship from having effective communication. Does your spouse build barriers that you would feel comfortable pointing out to them? Bringing down these barriers and clearing the path of communication is critical to a healthy marriage.

My husband and I spend countless hours trying to perfect our communication. At first, we took baby steps in learning how to talk to each other. At times, he can be demanding in a conversation, and I tend to want to control the outcome. This combination of communication styles brings with it a lot of work.

Early in our marriage, when we talked about finances, I immediately built a wall because I was the one preparing the budget. I carried the burden. He would innocently say he wanted something, and I would jump down his throat. It took us a while, but he's learned how to approach me with financial needs, and I've learned how to tell him of my financial fears. Together we opened up about our feelings, accepted criticism, and humbled ourselves when our pride wanted to rise up.

The Power Behind a Thought

A lot of what we say comes from what we think. If you are thinking about an upsetting comment your spouse made to you earlier that morning and they then ask how you feel, how will you answer? You will either have to make a conscious decision to lie, or you'll have to tell the truth. If we aren't careful in understanding the power of our thoughts, we may cause some unneeded arguments and disagreements with our spouse. Additionally, as we think positively, we will outwardly express those positive thoughts. Claiming victory with our words will keep our minds protected from negativity and fear.

Have you ever convinced yourself of something to the extent that it made you physically sick? Pondering negative thoughts can make us sick. People can see negativity on our faces and in our body language. Entertaining thoughts of fear, "what if," and anxiety can easily debilitate you until you can't cope. In essence, we can talk ourselves into depression if we're not careful. Realize the power in positive thinking along with the effects of negative thoughts. Your marriage needs you to be an uplifting and encouraging spouse. Your thoughts will direct your steps, and you'll become either a positive or negative spouse. Don't let the power of a positive mind go unused!

Surviving the Storms

Trials and storms are a part of all our lives. We must learn how to communicate during these storms so we can make it through them. Life's storms come in many shapes and sizes and are different for each marriage. Some families experience financial difficulties, job loss, death of a child, or health issues. We don't get to pick and choose what storms we want or don't want to go through. However, we can control how we choose to work with our spouse to get through the storm, to grow from the experience, and to grow closer because of it.

To work together through storms, we must communicate effectively and compassionately with our spouse. We must also keep our mind protected from fear, worry, and anxiety.

As a couple, you need to strengthen your marriage so you can deal with your storms, no matter their intensity. The stronger your marriage is before entering a storm, the less likely you will be to experience severe marital problems because of it.

Also, the more you communicate with your spouse during a trial, the more emotional support you can give each other. Don't isolate yourself or go into a comatose state when life's problems are at your doorstep. Instead, grab all the strength God and your spouse can offer.

During trials, we often feel vulnerable, especially if we are the one experiencing the health problem or the job loss. Protect your mind by sharing your emotions with your spouse so they can share your burden. Opening up in these situations can enhance your bond.

As you grow in compassion during storms, work at not being judgmental. Judging words will not draw you closer or strengthen your marriage. At times, one spouse may want to offer assistance to the other, but the hurting spouse may reject it. Be patient until they are ready to accept your help. Remain loving and keep communication flowing. When your spouse is ready to open up, take the time to listen.

As you go through the storm, keep communication open with God too. It takes time to learn to thank Him during a trial. However, it is crucial to refuse to entertain thoughts of blaming God. He is not out to get you. Good people experience bad things. We all will go through them at one level or another, so blaming God won't help.

Evaluate what you can get out of the experience. How can you grow closer to God during the trial? Thank Him for getting you through, even if you aren't through yet. Claim it, believe it, and let God know you trust Him. Thank Him for all that is going on in your life. He has much bigger plans for you than you could ever imagine! If you lose your job, look at it as a blessing, because maybe God has a new job lined up for you that makes more money or that you will love doing. If you experience financial difficulties, thank God. Maybe this trial is the final straw that will make you change your spending habits. It could be the eye-opener you've needed to gain financial freedom.

Keeping the helmet of communication on during all trials will protect your mind and your marriage. As your mind remains protected, you can keep your spouse encouraged and remain in love with God. You will not need to self-medicate for relief, and you will strengthen your marriage.

Spending Time

Spending time together is valuable in keeping communication alive in your marriage. This doesn't necessarily mean you have to talk. Communication can go way beyond the spoken word. Spending time without words is a form of communication that we all must remember to nurture from time to time. Imagine sitting in front of the fire, snuggling with your spouse. There's no need for words, because you both know what the other is thinking. You're enjoying time with the one you love.

Neglecting moments like these will have slow, negative consequences on your marriage. Life moves too fast, and often we work at "making it through" each day. The longer you neglect your marriage and the less quality time you spend with your partner, the more time and effort it will take to revive, if you're able to revive at all. Find moments to communicate without words. Making sure your spouse knows you love them unconditionally will protect their mind from negative thoughts. They won't wonder whether you are still interested in them or whether you still value their friendship or whether you're still attracted to them.

My husband and I spend time together playing tennis, remodeling the house, or even having him tickle my back as we watch television. All three of these activities communicate their own message to me. When he wants to do one of these things, I feel loved without him even having to say anything. Knowing he wants to take the time to play tennis and have fun means he's still my friend. He doesn't have to tell me that. I know because he asked me to do it.

When we remodel together, we feel productive and have fun doing it. Yes, it's definitely a sickness, but we love tearing our house apart and putting it back together. When we're doing this, I know that he believes I'm a good worker and that he appreciates what I do for our family. Again, he doesn't have to tell me. I know by his actions.

I hear stories about husbands and wives who don't spend time together, or when they do, it's always with the children. To keep nurturing the communication in your marriage and to help keep the love and intimacy alive, you must spend time together alone! Do this without feeling obligated to talk, but just to share the moments.

Intimacy

Intimacy and affection are critical pieces of a healthy marriage. They let your spouse know you love them and find them attractive. Knowing your spouse finds you attractive and enjoys showing you affection offers protection to the mind. Physical gestures can communicate love silently.

Physical affection generally fluctuates throughout the course of a relationship. When first married, most couples are affectionate because of overwhelming hormones. Your relationship is new and exciting, and you don't have children or a home or other demanding responsibilities. As your marriage matures, and the responsibilities in the household increase, the excitement of physical intimacy might slow down. It may be harder to find time and energy for physical intimacy. Homes, children, work, trials and storms, and health issues can affect the time you spend sharing physical intimacy. When this happens, make sure to keep affection at the forefront of your marriage. You can do this by finding other ways to show affection such as snuggling, holding hands while taking walks, hugging, giving massages, or kissing.

Do what you can to keep affection and intimacy alive in your marriage. First Corinthians 7:5 states, *"Do not deprive one another except with consent for a time that you may give yourselves to fasting and prayer; and come together again so that Satan does not tempt you because of your lack of self-control."*

This scripture makes it clear that we should satisfy our spouse's desire for intimacy and not neglect their needs. It also warns us that if we aren't fulfilling the sexual needs of our spouse, they might be tempted by another. I encourage you to meet your spouse's physical needs and keep them satisfied.

Taking the time to find creative ways to communicate your love will enhance your relationship as it has ours. I encourage you to learn to be affectionate in many different ways, including the written word. You may find a whole new side of your spouse that you didn't know existed when intimacy is expressed in words. When you expose a verbal aspect into your relationship, you strengthen the other

ingredients in your marriage. Be encouraging, inspiring, and show.

Finally, learn to be intimate with God. Sharpening this

relationship can substitute for the physical intimacy you're missing

from your spouse. It is fulfilling to realize the depths of God's love for

you. When you come to terms with how much He loves you,

reciprocate it back to Him. Especially when you're feeling lonely or

needy, take time out to spend with God. Focus on His love for you.

Think about the great things He has done for you. Find satisfaction in

the fullness of His love and your love for Him.

Where's Your Helmet?

The helmet of communication is a powerful piece of armor.

When you communicate regularly with your spouse, you won't have

any emotional surprises when they get home. Communication will keep

your mind and thoughts safe from fear.

A sound mind is crucial for building a strong Christian

marriage, but we often leave the house without our helmet of

protection. Our minds are often left open and vulnerable to attacks that

can severely affect our marriage. It doesn't take long each morning to ask God to keep our thoughts pure and positive. It doesn't take much effort to communicate with your spouse. Spend your day looking for God's goodness in what He has done for you. His love for you will yield a sound mind.

For God has not given us a spirit of fear, but of power and of love and of a sound mind. (2 Timothy 1:7)

Embrace the power behind your thoughts and use that power to enhance your marriage. Communicate often with your mate and make sure to listen to what they have to say. Work toward experiencing joy in your relationship like you have never had before. Think it! Believe it! Claim it!

TIME TO ENGAGE

The helmet of communication will protect your mind, but only if you remember to apply it. Open lines of communication will allow you both to grow together, not apart. Continue to learn about each other and dream together. Learn from the storms in your life. Spend quality time together. Don't hesitate to try new things to express your love for each other. Most important, don't let others quench your desire to spend time with the person you fell in love with.

Questions for Reflection

- Reflect on how well you and your spouse communicate. Do you have above-average communication skill, average, or below-average?

- What communication barriers affect your marriage the most? How can you help pull down those barriers?

- Do you struggle with negative thoughts bringing you down? If so, what can you do to turn your thoughts around?

- What are your favorite things to do with your spouse? What would you be doing if you were spending quality time together? What answer do you think your spouse would give?

- Spend time remembering certain trials you and your spouse have been through. What helped you through those storms? Did you learn things about your relationship as you went through them or once the storm was over?

A Call to Action

- Make a list of things you can do to improve communication with your spouse. Have your spouse do the same. Compare lists and work on implementing those ideas.

- Develop new ways to have quality time with your spouse. Ask your spouse to do the same. Compare your lists and implement some of your new ideas.

- Make a list of ways to increase the amount of physical affection in your marriage. Implement the ideas on your list.

- Ask your spouse how you could better meet their emotional and physical needs while making love.

Time with God

- 1 Corinthians 7:3: *"Let the husband render to his wife the affection due her, and likewise also the wife to her husband."*

- Proverbs 14:1: *"The wise woman builds her house, but the foolish pulls it down with her hands."*

- Matthew 24:43: *"But know this, that if the master of the house had known what hour the thief would come, he would have watched and not allowed his house to be broken into."*

- Mark 3:25: *"And if a house is divided against itself, that house cannot stand."*

- Ecclesiastes 3:1-2: *"To everything there is a season, a time for every purpose under heaven: a time to be born, and a time to die; a time to plant, and a time to pluck what is planted."*

CHAPTER SEVEN: THE SWORD

Focus Thought: The tongue is a sword that can easily edify someone or crush them completely.

Focus Verse: "Therefore comfort each other and edify one another, just as you also are doing" (1 Thessalonians 5:11).

Sword of Edification

The tongue is considered a sword because it can easily edify someone or crush them completely. When we edify someone, we instruct, or uplift them. Taming the tongue and choosing our words carefully will eliminate any chance of hurting others with our comments.

Be alert to the need to tame your tongue so you won't say something you'll regret later. Uplifting and comforting your spouse has a more positive effect than bringing them down or criticizing them.

How do you use your sword? Are you considerate of your spouse's feelings? Do you nag or bring your spouse down because they didn't meet one of your expectations? Realizing how you treat your spouse and those around you is the first step toward change.

Each of us has the capability, through our word choices, either to make someone's day or ruin it. We should carefully choose our words from the moment we wake up. The first words you say to your spouse will set the tone for the rest of your day. If you wake up early and spend time praying and getting right with God early in the morning, your words will likely be encouraging. However, if you wake up grumpy and spend no time asking for God's help, you will probably lash out at your spouse.

The sword we carry is a serious weapon. As you grow in Christ, you will learn to carry a sword of protection and edification, not one of destruction. I encourage you to reflect during this chapter and come up with ways to use your sword for edification. If you have trouble, you may need to look into your heart to see why you are unable to edify those around you. Check for built-up anger; it will prevent you from expressing love and speaking positive words. Your words reflect what is on the inside. It's hard to conceal hidden negativity. Be careful when you open your mouth.

A bit in the mouth of a horse controls the whole horse. A small rudder on a huge ship in the hands of a skilled captain sets a course in the face of the strongest winds. A word out of your

mouth may seem of no account, but it can accomplish nearly

anything—or destroy it! A careless or wrongly placed word out

of your mouth can do that. By our speech we can ruin the world,

turn harmony to chaos, throw mud on a reputation, send the

whole world up in smoke and go up in smoke with it. . . . This

is scary: you can tame a tiger, but you can't tame a tongue—it's

never been done. The tongue runs wild, a wanton killer. With

our tongues we bless God our Father; with the same tongues we

curse the very men and women he made in his image. Curses and

blessings out of the same mouth! (James 3:3-10)

Compassion

Uplifting includes showing compassion. Compassion fills you
with an intense desire to do whatever you can to help someone else. It
is also a tool that can help extinguish anger, motivate you to help your
spouse, or to help you understand a different perspective. If your heart
is not sensitive to the needs of others, it will be impossible to show
compassion. In marriage, we need to discern our spouse's need. When
you sense the need, it is important to show your spouse compassion

and love. They often need to hear words of encouragement. At times, showing compassion will require you to put your own feelings on the back burner.

Has your spouse ever treated you rotten when you were down? How did it make you feel? Maybe deep inside you were looking for one word of encouragement such as, "You are so talented," or "You look beautiful today." Instead, maybe you heard, "Why didn't you go grocery shopping?" or "Man, you look awful today!"

These statements probably caused much unneeded tension and anger in your household. Many arguments start because one spouse isn't in tune to the other's needs. A man might make comments without intending to hurt his wife, but because she needed encouragement, the effects of the comments were magnified. We must think through how we speak to each other.

If you struggle with compassion, you can pray to God to help you in that area. If you have a sincere heart, God will grant your desires. He will shine light on comments before you make them and let you know whether you should speak or remain silent. He may give you a gut feeling that you aren't treating someone right. Be careful! If you ask for it, God will give it! The truth He reveals can sometimes be hard to swallow. For years, I had a problem with being compassionate. Because I need to be in control, I tend to be cold when it comes to others' needs. As I prayed to God for help in this area, He showed me things about myself I did not like to see. However, it was worth it. I have been slowly changing as I've been growing in Christ. I find myself being more sensitive to others' needs, especially the needs of my husband. Making changes in yourself is difficult but rewarding. I encourage you to work at improving your level of compassion if this is an area you struggle with.

Respect

Respecting your spouse will encourage and uplift them. As your respect for them grows, you'll find it easier to listen to their needs and not rise up in anger or be confrontational. Respect is important in marriage. We often forget that as husband and wife, we are equal partners. If you allow yourself to show disrespect within your relationship, you dishonor your partner.

Our parents taught us an old saying while we were growing up: "Treat others as you would like to be treated." We all want to be treated with respect, so remember that when you start to fail in that area. If you find yourself disrespecting your spouse, find ways to apologize for your actions. Come humbly before the other if you mistreat them. Before you get to the point that you have to apologize, focus on your spouse's positive traits and show tolerance and patience with their faults.

For some, it may be easier to show respect to perfect strangers than to those they are closest to. Why do you think that is? We often let our guard down within the safety of our own home or within our circle of family and closest friends. During these times, we may not be as careful with our words or how we express ourselves. Don't be two different people: one when you're out in the world and another when you are home with your loved ones. Pray for consistency in your day.

Showing respect can also be challenging if you don't respect the person you are with. Take a moment to reflect about your spouse. Do you respect who they are? Do you respect the things they've accomplished or haven't accomplished? If we have difficulty respecting our husband or wife, should we pretend to show them respect? No; instead, drill deep to find any hidden reasons as to why you are unable to show consistent respect in your marriage. Do only certain times trigger moments of disrespect? Perhaps a pattern causes certain moments in which you are not as encouraging. Because of my high expectations, I tend to respect others to the degree in which my expectations have been met. Because I struggle with these expectations, I have to work harder each morning to give my control issues over to God.

It is important to respect the person you love. Encourage your husband or wife by respecting who they are. Be specific; praise them for their accomplishments or maybe for their consistency and faithfulness. Give time to hear their opinions. Marriage is a partnership, so we must learn to respect the partner we intend to spend the rest of our lives with.

Friendship

Maintaining a friendship takes work and must be a priority. Friendship in marriage is no different—it takes work. Offering friendship to your husband or wife is one of the most encouraging actions you can take to show your love. Simply letting your spouse know you need and desire their friendship will satisfy and uplift them.

I will never forget that before my husband and I were married, he told me he wanted to grow old with me. This was the first time he hinted at wanting a long-term commitment. That comment sent shivers down my spine in a way I will never forget. I knew at that moment how valuable our friendship was to him and that he didn't want to lose it. Even today, we talk about how we'll be ninety years old and still together, laughing like great friends. We say, "Neither of us will have teeth, but at least we'll have each other."

My friendship with my spouse is one of the things I cherish most about our relationship. I know he loves me, but I also know that I never want to lose his friendship. As you approach each day alongside your best friend, you can experience joy and satisfaction in all the things you do. As you go through trials with your best friend, you will have someone to lean against to help you get through them. Never underestimate the power of friendship in a marriage. I never want to lose that friendship with my husband.

If you have moments in which you are not encouraging, have started an argument, or have fueled the fire of an argument, remember that your friendship is suffering. Each time you argue or fail to encourage your spouse, you hammer a dent in your relationship. When my husband and I argue, the one thing that upsets me the most is that I feel as if I'm losing my friend.

Negative comments or hurtful actions can ruin a friendship, sometimes forever. Have you ever had a friendship end because of a disagreement? Friendships are lost because one or both parties are too stubborn to resolve the disagreement. We speak words that sever the relationship beyond repair. The tongue, your sword, is a powerful weapon. Don't let it destroy your friendships! Ask for daily strength from God to help you control your thoughts and your words. Spend time reminding yourself throughout your day that your words have a direct impact on everyone you speak to. Will you make friendships or will you break them?

Finally, don't let your friends or children take the place of your friendship with your spouse. Too often, we hear of marriages suffering because the husband or wife is closer friends with their children or their best buddy than with their spouse. The bond between husband and wife must be stronger and more solid than any other relationship outside of God. The parent-child relationship must be secondary to that between the husband and wife, or the spousal relationship will suffer. Keep proper order in your marriage: God first, spouse second, children third.

The Power of Goals and Dreams

When my husband appeared on NBC's *America's Got Talent* I stood backstage and watched him live his dream. It was one of the best experiences of my life! Though it wasn't my dream, I wanted my husband's music dream to come true. As he walked onstage in his military uniform and received a standing ovation, I felt so proud of him. He had sacrificed for his country in Iraq, and to see the audience appreciate him for that was priceless. When he started singing, the audience erupted! I have never seen my husband's face glow so intensely as that moment. He was living his dream, and I was there to witness it!

We drove home in separate cars for two and a half hours, from Dallas to Fort Hood. We talked on our cell phones the entire drive, laughing like little kids, remembering moments from the day, and reliving the entire experience. We were living the dream—his dream. This was one of the most meaningful moments of our marriage.

Two years ago, my husband helped me achieve my dream: a lake house. I never thought it would be possible to have a house on a lake. I grew up visiting a cottage on Fox Lake most of my childhood, and I wanted so badly to experience that memory every day on my own lake. My husband grabbed hold of my dream and kept us focused. He believed we could achieve that dream much earlier than I had expected. Today we own a lake house we can have friends and family over to enjoy. I believe this dream came true because my husband accepted my dream as his own.

I encourage you to discuss your mate's dreams with them. Become interested in their dreams, encourage them to obtain them, and pray that you can experience living their dream with them.

As you grow together, encouraging each other and setting goals, you'll gain momentum. Though you do these things together, it is also important to have independent goals. This is not selfish but is something we all need. Make sure your spouse has a clear understanding of your goals so they can help you achieve them.

Working together on family goals is also necessary for a happy relationship. If we don't set goals, we drift through our days, hoping something will happen. Write a game plan, describing how you intend to achieve your family's goals. Hold each other accountable.

Encouraging your spouse to dream and working toward family goals may sound difficult, but try it! You might ignite a new spark of life and hope that you've never before seen in your spouse!

A Sword on Display Only

Imagine being attacked by a vicious monster. You have been given a spectacular sword and trained in its use by the master. The monster stretches toward you in attack position. You go to draw the sword, but wait! You didn't bring it.

You didn't bring it because you left it on display at home. Dust has built up as the sword hangs on two hooks above the fireplace. What happens now? You are facing your attacker unarmed!

Let this example remind you not to leave yourself vulnerable to your attacker. We must learn not only to dust off our sword, but to carry it with us. God has trained us in its use. He wants us to remain prepared at all times to encourage those around us. If we are caught off guard, something hurtful may come out of our mouths. Or we may choose not to say anything at all to someone who needs encouragement.

We should try to reflect God's love by encouraging everyone we meet. Your thoughtfulness toward another may be the only love they have felt in days or even years. Imagine the impact you can have on your world with simply a positive and encouraging tongue! And don't neglect your spouse.

TIME TO ENGAGE

The sword of edification requires us to put aside hurtful thoughts and selfish feelings. Our words can encourage others; yet, in a quick motion, they can crush someone completely. If we are not conscious of our words, we can damage our relationship with our spouse. Be careful what you do with your sword! Once words leave your mouth, you can't take them back. In James 3:8-11, the tongue is described as an unruly evil, full of deadly poison, able to bless our God and curse men. What will come out of your mouth?

Questions for Reflection

- We have all said things we wish we could take back. When you had a moment like this, did you feel guilty for hurting your spouse? Has your spouse ever hurt you with their words?

- How does your treatment of your spouse affect their self-esteem or sense of worth? Would your spouse say you're a blessing to them?

- Come up with creative ways to encourage your spouse.

A Call to Action

- List some things you can do to protect your friendship with your spouse. Implement at least one of the items from your list before you finish reading this book.

- Make a list of goals you wish to obtain independently. Write a plan of action describing how you can obtain at least one of your goals. Discuss your list with your spouse.

- List your spouse's positive traits. As you find yourself dwelling on negative aspects, get out your list and remember the positive things you love.

A Time with God

- Ecclesiastes 4:9-12: *"Two are better than one, because they have a good reward for their labor. For if they fall, one will lift up his companion. But woe to him who is alone when he falls, for he has no one to help him up. Again, if two lie down together, they will keep warm; but how can one be warm alone? Though one may be overpowered by another, two can withstand him."*

- Matthew 7:4: *"'Or how can you say to your brother, 'Let me remove the speck from your eye'; and look, a plank is in your own eye?'"*

121

May the God of hope so fill you with all joy and peace in believing that

by the power of the Holy Spirit you may abound and be overflowing

with hope (Romans 15:13 AMP.)

Also by Caroline Jens

40 Days Couples Journal

Whole Armor of Marriage, Military Edition

Guide to Financial Wellness

Protected Dreams

Whole Armor Ministry

If this book has been helpful to your marriage, please e-mail a

testimonial to:

Caroline and Daniel Jens

info@wholearmorministry.com

www.wholearmorministry.com